The Rebirth of Music

LaMar Boschman

Destiny Image® **Publishers, Inc.**
P.O. Box 310
Shippensburg, PA 17257-0310

ISBN 0-914903-80-2

For Worldwide Distribution
Printed in the U.S.A.

Revised edition: 2000

This book and all other Destiny Image, Revival Press, MercyPlace, Fresh Bread, and Treasure House books are available at Christian bookstores and distributors worldwide.

For a U.S. bookstore nearest you, call **1-800-722-6774**.
For more information on foreign distributors, call **717-532-3040**.
Or reach us on the Internet: **http://www.reapernet.com**

Dedication

This book is dedicated to my partner in life and ministry, my wife, Teresa. Her tireless efforts, love, and prayer are an invaluable part of our ministry. For more than 25 years, we have pioneered together the truths of worship in our Lord's Church.

Contents

Introduction

Being involved in a ministry that teaches the importance of lifting up Jesus through music, I was excited after reading *The Rebirth of Music*. This book is packed with Scripture and concepts about music that the Church needs.

LaMar shares some very revealing Scripture regarding lucifer's (satan's) involvement in music before he fell from Heaven and his counterfeiting efforts since he has fallen.

Very simply, God is the creator of all things, and He intends for the Church to give light and leadership to the world. We as the Body of Christ can no longer allow the world to dictate the trends of music, but we must instead offer music that is unparalleled in power because of the creative power of God that dwells in us.

I highly recommend *The Rebirth of Music* to anyone involved in music ministry or anyone who simply wants to better understand music's role in our lives according to Scripture.

Phil Driscoll

Publisher's Foreword

Today, more than ever before, we are seeing the manifestations of lucifer's dominion. Charging ahead go the shock troops of his army, the myriads of musicians of this day. With lyrics of sensuous deception, rebellion, and the occult driven into the mind and body by the driving sound of instruments and amplifiers pushed to torturous, earsplitting levels, the message of lucifer's kingdom goes forth. Thousands give themselves in ecstatic worship before those emissaries of "the god of this age."

God be praised that the One who "sang" the worlds into existence, the true God of all eternity, the One who created music in the beginning is raising up a pure and shining army to stand against this onslaught. Armed with the two-edged sword of the Word and with the "high praises of God in their mouth," these praising men and women will go forth in the vanguard of the army as did the singers and dancers of Jehoshaphat's day. They will storm the very gates of hell, regain the lost dominion, and stand in the place vacated by lucifer's fall, leading the angelic hosts in everlasting praise and worship to the Most High God.

As LaMar Boschman shows in this book, such is the breadth and purpose of *The Rebirth of Music*.

The Publisher

Chapter One

Music, Angels, and Lucifer

Long before God made man or even formed the earth, as we know it today, He created an angel in the Third Heaven, giving him the ability to play music. In fact, this angel was made with instruments of music built into his body. He was a special celestial being—an archangel. No cherub or seraph was allowed to be closer to the throne of God than he. Only two other angels in Heaven came close to his position of authority and responsibility. These were the archangels, Michael and Gabriel.

Power Angels

Michael, a warrior and a protector, fought the principality called the Prince of Persia who opposed Daniel and his prayers.[1] Michael was one of the chief princes, the prince of Israel—the

---

1.   See Dan. 10:13.
2.   See Dan. 10:21.

heavenly patron and champion of Israel.[2] Michael also opposed the devil in the dispute over Moses' body.[3] In the Apocalypse, he leads the angelic armies in war against the old serpent, satan.[4] Some scholars believe that he may be the archangel that announces the coming of the Lord.[5]

The second archangel, Gabriel, is a messenger angel who was instructed to explain to Daniel the meaning of his vision.[6] It was Gabriel who told Zachariah and Elizabeth that they were going to bring forth a son who would prepare the way for the Messiah. Gabriel also appeared to Mary saying that she was highly favored among all the women on earth, and that she would bear a son, Jesus, who would be the Savior of the world.[7]

The third archangel was lucifer—the music angel. Ezekiel describes him: "You were in Eden, the garden of God; every precious stone was your covering....The workmanship of your timbrels and pipes was prepared for you on the day you were created" (Ezek. 28:13 NKJ).

Some scholars debate whether lucifer was in the Garden of Eden. However, this Scripture may not refer to the Garden of Eden in Genesis, but a metaphor of the presence of God. "The workmanship" is interpreted as "service," which is the meaning of the word *ministry*. He was given these music instruments in order to serve, not to use them for his advantage.

The Music Angel

Most theologians believe that lucifer had tambourines and pipes built into his body, and that he possessed the ability to play these instruments extremely well. It is very clear that lucifer excelled in music and that it was an actual part of him.

3.　See Jude 1:9.
4.　See Rev. 12:7.
5.　See 1 Thess. 4:16.
6.　See Dan. 8:16; 9:21.
7.　See Lk. 1:19,26.

The Bible refers to "pipes," plural, meaning there were more than one. The notes these pipes made were possibly harmonious, blending with one another. And since there were more than one, perhaps three, they could have made a chord.

The tabrets, or tambourines, another part of lucifer's body, gave him rhythm, a beat for the music that he played. In fact, within lucifer's makeup represented most categories of musical instruments that we have today—string, wind, and percussion. The pipes mentioned in Ezekiel 28:13 were a type of the wind instruments; the tambourines represented the percussion instruments. Lucifer was also able to make music on stringed instruments, as revealed in Isaiah 14:11-12:

> *Your pomp is brought down to Sheol, and the **sound of your stringed instruments**; the maggot is spread under you, and worms cover you. How you are fallen from heaven, O lucifer, son of the morning!* (NKJ, emphasis mine)

These stringed musical instruments were "viols" or a six-stringed instrument.[8] So the total spectrum of instruments that we play today, except for electronic instruments, were built into lucifer's body, and he could play them all.

Not only was lucifer a musician, but he was also the instrument as well. Lucifer didn't sit down at a piano; he *was* a piano! And he didn't carry a guitar around his neck; he *was* a guitar. Lucifer possessed this talent and the ability to play instruments, producing a sound in his service of worship to God.

According to *Strong's Exhaustive Concordance of the Bible*, lucifer's name means "light-bearer," "morning star," or "day star." He is also called by several other names, such as "Son of the Morning" and "the Anointed Cherub." Lucifer was given a definite anointing for serving or ministering in music. In Ezekiel 28:14,16,

---

8.   James Strong, *Strong's Exhaustive Concordance of the Bible* (Peabody, MA: Hendrickson Publishers, n.d.), **nebel** (#5035)—a harp, a lute, a guitar, a musical instrument.

the Bible says that lucifer dwelt in the mountain of God (possibly the presence of God) and was the covering cherub. God had created the angels to worship Himself, and it was lucifer's responsibility to lead all the angelic hosts in praise and worship to God the Father. He was Heaven's choir director, music minister, or worship leader.

And suddenly there was with the angel a multitude of the heavenly host praising God, and saying, Glory to God in the highest, and on earth peace, good will toward men (Luke 2:13-14).

I saw also the Lord sitting upon a throne, high and lifted up, and His train filled the temple. Above it stood the seraphim...And one cried unto another, and said, Holy, holy, holy, is the Lord of hosts: the whole earth is full of His glory (Isaiah 6:1-3).

Some scholars say that these "seraphim" were singing seraphs.

And I beheld, and I heard the voice of many angels round about the throne and the beasts and the elders; and the number of them was ten thousand times ten thousand, and thousands of thousands; saying with a loud voice, Worthy is the Lamb that was slain to receive power, and riches, and wisdom, and strength, and honour, and glory, and blessing (Revelation 5:11-12).

Because lucifer's responsibility was to lead the angelic hosts in singing and playing, he most likely provided the accompaniment on his pipes, tabrets, and viols. God had given him a special anointing for this powerful ministry in music. Lucifer was the master musician in Heaven. He very possibly was the choir director and the orchestra leader, as well as the entire orchestra.

In the beginning, music was created to minister to God the Father and to worship Him.[9] God birthed the ministry of music in lucifer to lead the angelic hosts in worship. It was ordained by God and was pleasing to Him. Any use of music other than worship to

9.   See Col. 1:16.

God is a violation of the purpose for which God created music. God did not create music for any secular purpose, and there was no secular music in the beginning. All music was *from God* and *for God* and part of the Kingdom of God. He did not even create music for evangelism. God created music for worship. Music can be used to reach the unsaved, but if that is all we use music for, we are living beneath our privilege and are not reaching a total spiritual fulfillment in music.

Lucifer was a worship leader, whom the Bible describes as being very wise and extremely beautiful—an awesome musical creature.

> *...every precious stone was thy covering, the sardius, topaz, and the diamond, the beryl, the onyx, and the jasper, the sapphire, the emerald, and the carbuncle, and gold...* (Ezekiel 28:13).

> *You were **blameless** in your ways from the day you were created till wickedness was found in you* (Ezekiel 28:15 NIV, emphasis mine).

> *Your heart became proud on account of your **beauty**, and you corrupted your **wisdom** because of your **splendor**...* (Ezekiel 28:17 NIV, emphasis mine).

Lucifer was an angel of light and radiated with brilliance. Everything about him was perfect from the day he was created.

> *Son of man, take up a lament concerning the king of Tyre and say to him: "This is what the Sovereign Lord says: 'You were the model of perfection, full of wisdom and perfect in beauty'"* (Ezekiel 28:12 NIV).

The Master Musician Rebels

Then one day in the midst of all the harmony, order, and divine music in Heaven, "when the morning stars [angels] *sang* together, and all the sons of God shouted for joy" (Job 38:7, emphasis mine), lucifer saw his own beauty and brilliance and became arrogant and lifted up in pride:

5

> *I **will** ascend into heaven, I **will** exalt my throne above the stars of God: I **will** sit also upon the mount of the congregation, in the sides of the north: I **will** ascend above the heights of the clouds: I **will** be like the most High* (Isaiah 14:13-14, emphasis mine).

Lucifer desired worship for himself. God could not allow this rebellion, so He removed lucifer out of the Third Heaven and cast him down to the earth. With him went a third of all the angels in Heaven, perhaps because he had tricked them into worshiping him. He may have desired worship so much that he conned these angels into worshiping him and becoming part of his following.

> *And there appeared another wonder in heaven....Michael and his angels fought against the dragon; and the dragon fought and his angels, and prevailed not; neither was their place found any more in heaven. And the great dragon was cast out, that old serpent, called the devil, and satan, which deceiveth the whole world: he was cast out into the earth, and his angels were cast out with him* (Revelation 12:3,7-9).

> *...I beheld satan as lightning fall from heaven* (Luke 10:18).

> *Through your widespread trade you were filled with violence, and you sinned. So I **drove you** in disgrace from the mount of God, and I **expelled you**, O guardian cherub, from among the fiery stones. Your **heart became proud** on account of your beauty, and you corrupted your wisdom because of your splendor. So I **threw you to the earth**; I made a spectacle of you before kings* (Ezekiel 28:16-17 NIV, emphasis mine).

Lucifer fell from the lofty position that he once held in the Third Heaven before the very presence of God. Satan's kingdom now fills the atmosphere around the earth, even to the very surface of the earth.

> *How you are fallen from heaven, O lucifer, son of the morning! How you are cut down to the ground, you who weakened the nations!* (Isaiah 14:12)

However, the Bible doesn't say that when God cast lucifer out of His presence that He took away his ministry of music, or his great ability to be wise. The day lucifer fell, music fell. Music that once was used to worship Almighty God now became music of an earthly nature; it became music of the world and began to appeal to our lower nature instead of appealing to God and our spiritual man (that part of us that has been born of God). Music, then, became corrupted. Music became used for self. Lucifer began to use it for his own worship and man for his own gratification. For the first time music became secular—outside the realm and reign of God.

The Bible suggests that there are worms in lucifer's music. "Your pomp [and] the music of your harps have been brought down to Sheol; Maggots are spread out [as your bed] beneath you, and worms are your covering" (Is. 14:11 NAS). Two kinds of maggots are among him—rapidly breeding ones[10] are under him, and voraciously devouring worms[11] cover him.

That anointed and powerful ministry of music that lucifer had in Heaven is now corrupted and cursed. It has a false anointing. Lucifer's music is now of the earth—earthly. His splendor has been brought down and is grossly debased. He fell, as well as his music. He still has that same powerful ministry to create worship, but now it is corrupted, and lucifer uses that ministry to entice worship for himself because he has an insatiable appetite for recognition, fame, reverence, and exaltation.

Lucifer wanted to achieve a higher position; he wanted to be number one; he wanted to be exalted above everything. Lucifer's desire was and is to receive worship for himself.

It is interesting to note the Arab legend that says the first song ever sung was the lament of Abel.[12] The first secular activity was

---

10.   *Strong's,* **maggot** (#7415)—as if rapidly breeding.
11.   *Strong's,* **maggot** (#8438)—as voracious, a crimson grub.
12.   A *lament* or a *dirge* is an expression of extreme grief or sorrow through chanting, wailing, or singing. There are many laments in the Old and New Testaments that were sung and accompanied by instruments.

the murder of Abel, and out of that came secular music. Music is often a part of man's sin. God, however, has always involved music with worship. Music was created by God for one main purpose and that is to exalt Him in worship.

Chapter Two

Music and Satan

Lucifer's association with music is a very profound and definite one. He had the ability to make any sound he wanted. As we have seen, he was not only a musician, but in Ezekiel 28:13 and Isaiah 14:11, we discover that lucifer had the ability to make music from his very being, which was made up of instruments. These instruments—the viols, tambourines, and pipes—were built in him the day he was created. Then he fell.

Lucifer's Lust

Lucifer was the music minister in Heaven, but he wasn't satisfied. He wanted to be the pastor. So he rebelled against the divine authority that was placed over him and caused a church split. Any church or group of Christians who rises against the authority God has placed over them may come under the influence of the same mentality and rebellious spirit lucifer had. He wanted *his* way, and thinking only of himself, he made a power play. That same "luciferian" mentality is among some believers today. Lucifer wanted his own following, his own worshipers. And lucifer today is still trying to entice people to bow down and worship him.

Even in Jesus' day lucifer was hungry for worship. One day just before Jesus was to enter into His ministry, satan, who most scholars believe used to be called lucifer, came to tempt Him. One of the things satan asked Jesus to do was to fall down at his feet and worship him:

> *Again the devil took Him to a very high mountain and showed Him all the kingdoms of the world and their splendor. "All this I will give You," he said, "if You will bow down and worship me"* (Matthew 4:8-9 NIV).

Satan claims to rule all worlds and kingdoms, in the cosmos and on earth. He attempted to bluff Jesus into submitting to him. "The temptation was threefold: to gain a temporal, not a spiritual, dominion; to gain it at once; and to gain it by an act of homage to the ruler of this world, which would make the self-constituted Messiah the vice-regent of the devil and not of God."[1]

Lucifer was saying, "You don't have to go to the cross to set up a kingdom. I'll give all the kingdoms of the world to You right now. You can take a shortcut, Jesus. I'll make You popular. I'll make You Jesus Christ Superstar. Everyone will know You because You will own all these kingdoms." But Jesus said to satan, "'Away from Me, satan! For it is written: "Worship the Lord your God, and serve Him only."' Then the devil left Him, and angels came and attended Him" (Mt. 4:10-11 NIV).

Even though satan couldn't convince *Jesus* to worship him, he still tries to get people to worship him today. He is still looking for worshipers. This is lucifer's lust.

Today, lucifer offers musicians the same proposition he offered Jesus. He offers the "kingdoms of this world" and the glory

---

1. McNeile from Robertson's *Word Pictures in the New Testament*, (Biblesoft, 1996).

and glamour of them to musicians, hoping they will get people to worship him through them. Lucifer says, "I'll give you my ability, I'll give you my ministry of music, if you will help me. I will anoint you with my anointing if you will just worship me. I will make you a superstar."

Some singers and musicians today have sold their souls so they can become superstars and have anything they want in the world. Some of these musicians waste their lives and resources on sin and debauchery—a self-centered luciferian lifestyle. Satan is working behind the scenes, manipulating, influencing, and setting up some of these situations through his demons and devils.

The song that comes from the heart and soul of these musicians is purely of the flesh and in some cases is of darkness. The inspiration is not from God; it is from the world, the flesh, or the devil. The spirit of the song can be sensual or dark, yet that song becomes a colossal hit, and the group is catapulted into superstardom. People flock to concerts and as soon as the bands step on stage, tens of thousands of people jump to their feet and begin singing, raising their hands, and dancing around. Lucifer has influenced people to sing and dance before him as he hides behind the groups and uses them to receive his worship. Most of the time it is just in fun that the fans express themselves. Yet in some cases there is much more going on than that—violence, lust, profanity, and explicit sex.

Spirituality is in today. Most boomers and busters want to connect with the other side. Witchcraft, New Age, and spiritism of all kinds are enjoying popularity. There are many superstar groups and music idols today that pray to a higher power before their concerts. Some pray directly to lucifer. A few music groups in the United States, and other parts of the world, blatantly give the credit for their ability and their stardom to lucifer, or satan. They worship him; they show him homage, and exalt him as a god. There are examples of this today on radio, television, and recordings. There is little doubt that satan has manipulated artists and groups into worshiping him and singing songs about him, giving glory to himself.

The Satanic Strategy

The Seattle-based alternative rockers Pearl Jam helped elevate despair, hopelessness, rebellion, and suicide to a new level. Even the media remarked about the band's bleakness. On the CD *No Code? No Way!* they changed their tunes to a more optimistic attitude. Perhaps the suicide of grunge pioneer Kurt Cobain the same year woke them up to the result this kind of music can bring. We must remember, it is not just the music, but the attitude, the spirit, and the circumstances that influence the listener toward sin and degradation.

In addressing the Pharisees, a Jewish religious group, Jesus stated that although they may be natural descendants of Abraham, they were not his spiritual descendants, because they were influenced and used by their spiritual father, the devil:

> *You belong to your father, the devil, and you want to carry out your father's desire. He was a **murderer from the beginning**, not holding to the truth, for there is **no truth in him**. When he lies, he speaks his native language, for **he is a liar** and the **father of lies*** (John 8:44 NIV).

Jesus teaches that the nature of the devil is that of killing and lying. The name satan means "to lie in wait, adversary." He is a deceiver. He obscures himself behind the obvious, waiting to steal, kill, and destroy.

Trent Reznor, of Nine Inch Nails, sings of bleak descent into pain and despair in a song called "Downward Spiral," which is a promotion of suicide.

"He put the gun to his head BANG!
So much blood for such a tiny hole.
Problems do have solutions,
A lifetime of XXXX things up,
Solved in one determined flash."

What a deception! Nothing is solved when we commit suicide. If one does not know Christ, his problems only get worse when he takes his life. Hell is a real place of torment and pain.

His Satanic Majesties Request

Have you ever wondered why groups focus and fixate on death, vulgarity, distorted truth, sex, violence, and anything else that is dark? They will name their group something extreme that attracts attention even though it may be dark and in your face. "Incubus," for example, the name of a popular rock group at the turn of the millenium, is an evil spirit that comes to women when they sleep to have sexual intercourse. Why aren't the names of groups wholesome and filled with light that speak of things pure, lovely, right, and decent? There is an evil force working in the hearts of men, which is the same force that Jesus said was working in the religious Pharisees—the devil, who is a murderer and liar.

There is an active power that causes evil to be more alluring to us than goodness, and the more evil it is, the more appealing it is. The more sensual it is, the more it relates to the baser nature of man. Sex sells because it appeals to the sex drive, which is one of the strongest drives God put in man, second perhaps to hunger. Humans desire these things because there is a basic nature in man that is earthly and is attracted to these fleshly, evil ideas and notions. This is very evident in music.

Many groups today give attention and glory to satan. Their CDs in the popular culture flaunt sex, and exploit evil and violence. Serpents and satanic influences appear on the record jacket as well as in the recorded product.

Several decades ago, Nazareth released two albums entitled *Hair of the Dog* and *Expect No Mercy*, which featured demon manifestations on the covers. On Savoy Brown's album, *Hellbound Train*, are examples of demonic art with pictures depicting satan. Satanic and spiritual influence is real and definite. The trend has not diminished even today. Why is that? The father of this world, satan, is behind the obvious deceiving and manipulating. Lucifer has the ability to make music; he still has a powerful ministry that is corrupt and evil, and you can see his influence today more than ever.

When some hard-core groups come out on stage, they perform as grossly as possible with their bodies, and speak as vulgarly as they can, to get a response from the audience who feels an identity with that violence and vulgarity. On television, I have seen excerpts of live concerts of groups who simulated sexual acts while playing their instruments. Old rockers like Mick Jagger and Dave Bowie often used to pretend to commit sex acts. Their performance was centered around sexual perversion. Music exposes the heart and spirit of the musician. Perhaps that is why it has been reported that they have had sex with their fans in numerous cities—that is what is in their hearts.

There is no doubt that this type of music is appreciated by the devil, especially when the group or artist actually sings about him in their lyrics. Fans think they are simply worshiping the superstars. Actually, they are worshiping lucifer, the spirit behind them.

God's Word says, "I urge you, brothers, in view of God's mercy, to offer your bodies as living sacrifices, holy and pleasing to God—this is your spiritual act of worship" (Rom. 12:1 NIV). Yes, our bodies are to be a sacrifice of worship, received as holy by God, not as a dark sex sacrifice to other gods.

Mick Jagger, lead singer of the Rolling Stones, once said, "I deliberately present myself as the personification of the devil."[2] Leon Russel preached, sang, and boogied with enough spiritual power to make his entire audience stand, jump, and dance in frenzied delight.

In Miami, Florida, before 14,000 people, the late Jim Morrison (formerly of the Doors) performed with such perversion and indecency that he was arrested and put in jail. The average age of

---

2.   Bob Larson, *Rock* (Wheaton, IL: Tyndale House, 1980), 44.

the audience was 12 to 14 years old. When asked why he did it, he said, "When I'm performing, I'm spiritual."

In the *Hotel California* album by the Eagles, they sing the song, "One of These Nights," describing the singer searching for the devil's daughter, who possesses demons and sexual desires. Bob Larson, in his book, *Rock*, points out in the song, "Undercover Angel," how well subtlety is used to bring out occult themes through music. The singer speaks in the song of a "midnight fantasy" to whom he makes love in bed. On the surface it seems like simply a bad dream. However, the song is based on the occult phenomenon of succubus, the cohabitation of a human male with a materialized demon spirit that assumes female proportions.

Jim Steinman admits, "I have always been fascinated by the supernatural and always felt rock was the perfect idiom for it."[3] The lead singer of the group says that when he is on stage he "gets possessed."

One of the boldest groups displaying evil in their presentations is the Rolling Stones. A record album entitled *Their Satanic Majesties Request* spells it out pretty clearly. Their song, "Sympathy for the Devil," has been chosen as an unofficial national anthem for satanists. Another song portraying satan worship is "Goat's Head Soup," which was recorded at an actual Haitian voodoo ritual. Behind the song you can hear the screams of people becoming possessed with evil spirits. Most people are not aware that the goat's head is the universal symbol of satan worship, but the Stones are.

Music can be a medium or doorway to spiritually move to the other side. Music from the dark side, manipulated by the enemy, is also spiritual music. Just as God requires music in our worship to Him, lucifer will use the same means to stir people for his spiritual purpose. Lucifer can create a spiritual atmosphere and release an evil unction upon the presentation of music, just as God dwells in our praises and the Holy Spirit comes upon us.

---

3.   *Rock*, 43.

True Worship Versus Dishonest Worship

God has ordained His people to worship Him by singing and praising, lifting up their hands unto the Lord, and even dancing before His name. The devil lures people to do those same things in worship to him. Why? Satan desires the same worship. However, unlike God, he is not a creator; he is a counterfeit, a copier, a deceiver. Whom are we worshiping in our music?

Lucifer is a deceiver and searches for worship just as God desires worship. But whereas God seeks true worshipers who worship Him in spirit and truth (see Jn. 4:24), lucifer looks for dishonest worshipers who worship him in spirit and deceit, evil, darkness, sensuality, and vulgarity.

Lucifer was given a powerful ministry of music, to worship within the highest regions of Heaven. He did not carry pipes around his neck or a tambourine in his hand; they were built into his body. But today he is fallen. That same ministry he had is now a powerful negative force. Moreover, as satan is being pressed closer and closer to the earth, and his time draws nearer and nearer to an end, he is feeling more and more threatened. Nevertheless, lucifer is wise and uses his strongest weapon, the thing that he can do best, what he has been doing ever since he was created—making music.

Satan is slowly deceiving those who don't understand the influence the spirit of some music and dance has. God wants us to be alert to the enemy's craftiness and his sneaky tactics.

Stand therefore, having your loins girt about with truth... (Ephesians 6:14).

God wants us to know truth, to be surrounded by truth. God wants believers to be wise to satan's trickery and treachery and to be prepared for more, for we have not yet seen the full potential that the spirit of some music will have in the world through his influence.

Chapter Three

Music and Its Importance

There are many references in the Bible to music—1028 to be exact. God must consider music very important to mention it that many times and to make it one of the major emphases in His Word. Each reference is there for a reason. Let us look at the importance and purpose of music.

Music and the Presence of God

Psalm 100:2b says, "Come before His presence with *singing*" (emphasis mine). This Scripture implies that God has a preference as to how He is approached.

If I were to appear before the President of the United States, I'd be expected to conduct myself in a manner that would show respect. There would be certain manners and courtesies that I would be expected to exhibit, a protocol that would be fitting for the President of the United States. The President of presidents, the King of kings, and the Lord of lords says, "To come into My presence, I want you to come rejoicing with music." Of all the ways God could choose for His people to come into His presence, He chose singing. We aren't supposed to come repenting or screaming confessions. The instruction is, "Come before His presence with singing."

Churches throughout the world are discovering how to enter the presence of God with musical praise: "Let us come before Him with thanksgiving and extol Him with *music* and *song*" (Ps. 95:2 NIV, emphasis mine).

The Bible says, "Enter His gates with thanksgiving, [and] His courts with praise. Give thanks to Him; bless His name" (Ps. 100:4 NAS). We sing songs of thankfulness to God, telling Him how thankful we are for all He has done for us. Then we enter into His courts with praise and begin to praise Him verbally, telling Him how much we love Him. The Bible informs us that God dwells in the praises of His people.

Psalm 22:3 says, "But You are holy, enthroned in the praises of Israel" (NKJ). Other translations say, "inhabits the praises of Israel" or "enthroned amid the praises of Israel." We, the Church, are spiritual Israel,[1] and God wants to dwell in our praise. Praise is birthed in music. The word *praise* here is a musical term. It means a song or hymn of praise. God dwells in, is enthroned on, the songs of praise that His people sing. God wants to be where the personal, vocal praise music is.

Musicians Wanted!

David received the greatest revelation of the importance of music in the house of the Lord in all the Scriptures. He set priests and Levites in the house of the Lord whose sole purpose was to provide music. They were to minister before God with singing and with instruments of music.

---

1. See Gal. 6.

*And these are they whom David set over the **service of song** in the house of the Lord, after that the ark had rest. And they ministered before the dwelling place of the tabernacle of the congregation with **singing**, until Solomon had built the house of the Lord in Jerusalem: and then they waited [served] on their office according to their order* (1 Chronicles 6:31-32, emphasis mine).

David appointed these priests to look after the "service of song" or "song service." Song is for the purpose of serving the Lord. It is a ministry or "service of song" to God. It must have been a very important part of the service in the tent of David, because these singers didn't work at any other job. They were on full-time staff to minister music in the house of the Lord. They were paid from the tithes of the people, given a place to stay on the church property, and were always available to minister.

*And these are the **singers**, chief of the fathers of the Levites, who remaining in the chambers were free: for they were employed in that work day and night* (1 Chronicles 9:33).

*Of the sons of Asaph, the singers were over the business of the house of God. For it was the king's commandment concerning them, that a certain portion should be for the **singers**, due for every day* (Nehemiah 11:22b-23).

*And he had prepared for him a great chamber, where aforetime they laid the meat offerings, the frankincense, and the vessels, and the tithes of the corn, the new wine, and the oil, which was commanded to be given to the Levites, and the **singers**, and the porters; and the offerings of the priests* (Nehemiah 13:5).

The ministry of music is as important as any other ministry in the house of the Lord. The singers were part of the ministry staff of the Church in the Old Testament. They were not to provide special music, but to help lead in worship and sing and make music to God.

Role of Music in Public Worship

The musical part of a worship service is not a mere preliminary, something that we should hurry through so that we can get

19

to the more important part of the service. It's not an icebreaker; it's not something to get people warmed up with. A church service isn't a party.

Musical worship is a prerequisite for the Word. Music prepares us to receive the sermon or the Word of the Lord. We should come to minister (worship) to the Lord. It will knit our hearts together in love and bring down the barriers between us and God, enabling Him to minister to us. The Holy Spirit can flow out and purify us when we come into His presence. Music has the ability to break down barriers, open our spirits, and soften our hearts.

Music prepares us to receive the Word. In Second Kings 3, there is an account of Jehoshaphat, king of Judah, and the kings of Israel and Edom wanting help and direction from the Lord. They had journeyed seven days from home and had run out of water needed for all their animals and the servants who traveled with them. Having heard that Elisha was a prophet of the Lord, they went to ask him for the word of the Lord. The first thing Elisha did was call for a minstrel (a player of a stringed instrument) and ask him to play. On this occasion, Elisha needed the ministry of music to prophesy.

After the minstrel had played, the "hand" of the Lord came upon Elisha and gave him a prophetic utterance, or the "word" of the Lord. Here we see the importance of music in preparing the way for the word. The first thing Elisha said was, "Bring me a minstrel." The Bible says that when the minstrel played, the hand of the Lord came upon Elisha, and he spoke very clearly the word of God. When the musician played, God moved. There was some divine activity that occurred when music was engaged.

Singing Is to Be Part of Our Daily Worship

Music is so important that God commanded it to be part of our daily lives as well as part of our worship to Him. The Bible says, "*Sing* unto the Lord, all the earth" (Ps. 96:1b, emphasis mine). The whole world is to sing to Him. Again, we are instructed to "*Sing unto the Lord with thanksgiving*" (Ps. 147:7a, emphasis mine).

Also, "...be filled with the Spirit; speaking to yourselves in *psalms* and *hymns* and *spiritual songs, singing* and making *melody* in your heart to the Lord" (Eph. 5:18-19, emphasis mine).

There are over 200 Scriptures that tell us to sing, which are too many to list here, but I think God is trying to tell us something. Do you suppose He likes music? It must be important to God because He mentions it so often. God loves to hear His Bride sing those beautiful love songs that are like a sweet perfume to Him—the songs of praise, which are the fruit of our lips. To God, music is important. It has a definite place in worship to the One we love. The ministry of music is a powerful entity that God wants to restore to its fullest potential because the Church has never before in its history flowed in the full capacity that God wants it to in the ministry of music.

The Strength of Praise and Worship

Just as we discussed in previous chapters, lucifer is getting stronger and stronger in the area of music. But God is raising up singers and musicians who are worshipers and know the theology of music and can step into the power ministry of music as Kingdom musicians. Because God considers music important, it is imperative today that we become part of the ministry of music in the Kingdom of God. The worshiping singers and musicians whom God is raising up will be sent forth into spiritual war when they praise. They will go into combat against the enemy with worship. And some of that warfare will be through music. The devil trembles at the sound of praises of God's people for two reasons: First, it reminds him of the place he once had in worship before God; second, when we praise, God's presence is revealed among us. Demons are driven back. The ministry of music is a powerful weapon that we can wield against the onslaught of the enemy.

These are exciting days we live in. We are seeing God restoring biblical praise and worship to His Church. It excites me to see praise and worship perfected through music and the ministry of music perfected through praise and worship, for the Bible promised a generation would be created that shall praise the Lord.[2] I'm glad that I'm a part of that generation to know and understand that music is important to God. Why else would God go to such care and attention to list so many songs in the Bible? The longest book in the Bible is God's songbook—the Book of Psalms. Music is important to God.

God Sings

"The Lord thy God in the midst of thee is mighty; He will save, He will rejoice over thee with joy; He will rest in His love, He will joy over thee with singing" (Zeph. 3:17). The Revised Standard Version says, "He will exult over you with loud singing." God rejoices over us with singing. Is this a mystical metaphor, or does God actually sing? What does He sound like? He must like music.

Jesus also sings and He proclaims in Hebrews 2:12b, "In the midst of the church will I sing praise unto Thee." Because of the importance music is given in the Old and New Testaments, I believe that God the Father, Jesus the Son, and the Holy Spirit love music. All three of the persons of the Godhead are mentioned in the Bible as singing.[3] Therefore, music, of necessity, must be considered important by us.

---

2.   See Ps. 102:18.

3.   God sings in Zephaniah 3:17; Jesus sings in Hebrews 2:12; and the Holy Spirit is mentioned as being involved in creating songs in Ephesians 5:19 (found in the term, "spiritual songs"—in the Greek, *ode pneumatikos*).

Chapter Four

Music and the Presence of God

There is a dimension of music that opens the door to the divine presence of God—it is praise and worship music. If our music is to be potent with the power of God, then we must know how to get past the execution of a song and worship God. Our music then becomes supernatural by the presence of God or the Holy Spirit.

Most music is performed to impress or to move others emotionally. Christian music that is "horizontal" can impress and stir people; however, if the only reason for using it is to display talent and move emotions, we are doing it with the wrong motive. Music of the Kingdom of God is spiritual music and goes beyond an admirable performance.

In the Old Testament, when a king or priest was to take office, he was anointed; that is, oil was poured upon his head,[1] and he was

---

1.   See Ex. 29:7.

set apart to God. In Exodus 28:41, God told Moses, "So you shall put them on Aaron your brother and on his sons with him. You shall anoint them, consecrate them, and sanctify them, that they may *minister to Me as priests*" (NKJ, emphasis mine). God wants musicians who are anointed and set apart for the ministry of music in the Kingdom of God, and whose sole purpose is to minister to the Lord.

Kingdom Musicians

Then the Lord spoke to Moses, saying: "Take the Levites from among the children of Israel and cleanse them ceremonially. Thus you shall do to them to **cleanse them**: *sprinkle water of purification on them, and let them shave all their body, and let them wash their clothes, and so* **make themselves clean**....*And you shall bring the Levites before the tabernacle of meeting, and you shall gather together the whole congregation of the children of Israel. So you shall* **bring the Levites before the Lord**, *and the children of Israel shall* **lay their hands on the Levites;** *and Aaron shall* **offer the Levites before the Lord**, *like a wave offering from the children of Israel, that they may perform the work of the Lord. Then the Levites shall lay their hands on the heads of the young bulls, and you shall offer one as a sin offering and the other as a burnt offering to the Lord, to make atonement for the Levites....Thus you shall separate the Levites from among the children of Israel, and the Levites* **shall be Mine**" (Numbers 8:5-7,9-12,14 NKJ, emphasis mine).

The Levites in David's Kingdom were responsible to sing before the Lord continually. "And these are the singers, chief of the fathers of the Levites, who remaining in the chambers were free: for they were employed in that work day and night" (1 Chron. 9:33).

"The Levites shall be Mine," God said. The Lord wants the musicians to be His, obedient and submitted to the will of the King, set apart as Kingdom musicians, to make music for God's pleasure.

"David spake to the chief of the Levites to appoint their brethren to be the *singers* with *instruments of music, psalteries* and *harps* and *cymbals*, sounding, by lifting up the voice with joy" (1 Chron. 15:16, emphasis mine). The sons, brothers, or male relatives of the leading Levites were instructed and trained to sing and play instruments in sacred music before the Lord.

> *For by the last words of David the Levites were numbered from twenty years old and above: because their office was to wait on the sons of Aaron for the service of the house of the Lord, in the courts, and in the chambers, and in the purifying of all holy things, and the work of the service of the house of God...And* **to stand every morning to thank and praise the Lord,** *and* **likewise at even;** *and to offer all burnt sacrifices unto the Lord in the sabbaths, in the new moons, and on the set feasts, by number, according to the order commanded unto them,* **continually before the Lord** (1 Chronicles 23:27-28, 30-31, emphasis mine).

The Levites from 20 years old and upward numbered 38,000, of whom 24,000 oversaw the work of the house of the Lord; 6,000 were officers and judges; 4,000 were doorkeepers; and 4,000 were musicians. One of their main functions was to "thank" (*yadah*—throw up their hands and worship) and "praise" (*halal*—to rave and boast of God to the point of looking like a madman). David drastically altered the worship of this period in Israel's history.[2]

Musicians of the Presence

God wants to pour the presence of the Holy Spirit on every minister and priest ministering in the house of the Lord, which includes singers and musicians. Without the presence of the Holy Spirit in our lives and ministries, we have nothing to offer except mere words. But when singers and musicians abide in the presence of God, great things happen.

The presence of God was above the mercy seat on the Ark of the Covenant. When the Ark was to be moved, it was the Levites' responsibility to do so. "And it came to pass, when God helped the

---

2. *International Standard Bible Encyclopaedia*, Electronic Database (Biblesoft, 1996).

Levites that bare the ark of the covenant of the Lord, that they offered seven bullocks and seven rams" (1 Chron. 15:26). The responsibility to carry the Ark of the Covenant and to transport the presence of God rested on the shoulders of the musical Levites. Likewise, today it is the musician's burden to escort the presence of God in, through the music he plays. The responsibility to carry the presence of God sits on the shoulders of the singer and player, as it did on the Levites.

In Solomon's temple on dedication day when the singers played, the glory of God so filled the temple that the priests couldn't stand to minister.[3] The Levites, the singers in verse 12, were worshipers who invoked the presence of God. The passion of worship of God was in their music. Verse 13 says, "It came even to pass, as the *trumpeters* and *singers were as one*, to make *one sound* to be heard in praising and thanking the Lord; and when they *lifted up their voice* with the *trumpets* and *cymbals* and *instruments of music*, and praised the Lord, saying, For He is good; for His mercy endureth forever: that then the house was filled with a cloud, even the house of the Lord."

The singers and musicians were in unity. They were all together making one musical sound. There were unified musically, spiritually, and in one worship voice. They were working together, flowing together in pure praise, so much so "that the priests could not stand to minister by reason of the cloud: for the glory of the Lord had filled the house of God" (vs. 14). The power and presence of God manifested as they worshiped in music.

How do we become musicians who have the power and presence of God on their music? The answer is simple: Pray and worship. Jesus touches us with His presence as a result of our worship music. We must ask the Holy Spirit through prayer to guide us to know what songs to play and what songs to sing, and to saturate and fill every song and every singing heart with the Lord's presence. Then can we truly minister to those who hear our music.

---

3. See 2 Chron. 5:12-14.

For His Eyes Only

Too many worship leaders in churches today, when leading in worship, pick favorite or popular songs, instead of asking God what He would like for His people to sing. There is nothing wrong with singing popular or favorite songs, but let's not ask each other our favorites; instead, let's ask God, before the service begins, what songs He wants us to sing. Worship is for His pleasure, not ours.

God has a purpose and a desire for every service. We should not gather just for the sake of having a church service; that ritual soon becomes religion. We gather to worship the King of kings and Lord of lords and to receive and to respond to what God wants to say to us in the service. We should seek the mind of the Lord when we enter a service to know what God wants to accomplish there. Just as much as the minister who is to preach the Word studies, prays, and asks God what he should preach, so the worship leader should ask God what songs to use to lead the people in worship.

It is very important as a musician, singer, worship leader, choir or orchestra leader to learn to flow in worship. It is difficult to know exactly what God is saying in the meeting when a service is choppy and the songs jump from one topic to another with no theme. A common theme keeps the service from being disjointed or lacking coherence.

The flow of a service is managed by everyone, including the pastor, worship leader, choir director, orchestra leader, singers, players, and the congregation, praying and seeking God. Often the songs sung in worship bring the glory and the conviction of the Holy Spirit upon the people in such a way that the altar call is given before the sermon is ever preached. Why does this happen? The presence of the Lord is revealed, touching hearts and lives. There is a theme and a purpose all the way through. The flow of a service is absolutely essential if we want God to use the service to its maximum potential. Without the presence of God and smooth transitions, the meeting becomes disorderly and often lifeless.

The Rebirth of Music

If we are together, in one accord, lifting up our voices with one sound to worship and praise the Lord, there is unity. Singers and musicians ought never to sing or play without having first prayed to God to anoint their instrument or music. If they do, their singing or playing will be simply nice music that cannot be used to its maximum potential. God wants us to be filled with the holy presence of His Spirit when we sing and minister in music. It is not talent that breaks the yoke over people's lives and sets the captive free. It is not great musical ability that brings God's glorious power. It is God's Spirit and presence that makes the difference in music ministry.

Not by might, nor by power, but by My spirit, saith the Lord of hosts (Zechariah 4:6b).

Chapter Five

Music and the Prophetic

In the Word of God there is a close association between music and prophecy. For example, many Scriptures of the Old and New Testaments were sung by the Holy Spirit-inspired ancient prophets. Many of the prophecies were not spoken or written, but were originally uttered with melodies. Some of these prophecies were delivered with the accompaniment of musical instruments. Music is associated with the intuitive and mystical dimensions of prophecy.

Throughout the Bible, there is a close relationship between music and the prophetic. Many of the psalms are considered to be prophetic. The Book of Psalms is a collection of songs written during a long period of time extending from Moses to the post-exile era of the second temple. Seventy-three songs in the Book of Psalms were written by David, twelve by Asaph, ten by the sons of Korah, two by Solomon; and Moses, Heman, and Ethan each wrote one. These songs were recorded as part of the Holy Scriptures because of the prophetic content in them.

Prophetic Songs

Prophecies about the coming Messiah being fulfilled in Jesus Christ were numerous. It is very possible that these powerful prophecies were sung.

Here is a list of some of these prophetic songs:

PROPHETIC SONG	SUBJECT	SONG FULFILLED
Psalm 2:7	Declared the Son of God	Matthew 3:17
Psalm 110:4	To be a priest	Hebrews 5:5-6
Psalm 41:9	Betrayed by a friend	Luke 22:47-48
Psalm 35:11	Accused by false witness	Mark 14:57-58
Psalm 35:19	Hated without reason	John 15:24-25
Psalm 22:7-8	Scorned and mocked	Luke 23:35
Psalm 69:21	Given vinegar and gall	Matthew 27:34
Psalm 109:4	Prayer for His enemies	Luke 23:34
Psalm 22:17-18	Soldiers gambled for His coat	Matthew 27:35-36
Psalm 34:20	No bones broken	John 19:32-33,36
Psalm 16:10	To be resurrected	Mark 16:6-7
Psalm 49:15	To be resurrected	Mark 16:6-7
Psalm 68:18	His ascension to God's right hand	1 Corinthians 15:4; Ephesians 4:8

King David and the others who sang those songs were moved upon by the Holy Spirit and the result was inspired music. Even though the canon of Holy Scriptures is complete and closed, the prophetic mantle that was upon these biblical songwriters can be upon musicians and songwriters today, who are singing songs of prophecy in churches of various denominations and fellowships.

I have personally experienced this expression of "spirit song." God has given me several songs of prophecy, some of which are now included in hymnbooks. What a joy it is when you feel that prophetic unction come upon you. Prophetic songs do not have to come only in the form of a full-length song, as such, with three verses and a chorus. They can also come as Scripture songs, and be of any length.

An example of this is the song I sang as a prophecy in a small church in Calgary, Alberta: "The Lord reigneth, the Lord reigneth.

Blessed be the name of the Lord, for the Lord our God, omnipotent, reigneth in majesty." That song, "The Lord Reigneth," is included in some hymnbooks today. Initially, it came to me as an impression from the Lord in the middle of spontaneous worship. When the praise quieted, I sang it out. Later, Integrity Music recorded it and it has touched many denominations.

Prophetic Musicians

David being a musician himself knew the place that the ministry of music should have in spiritual worship. He set aside whole families to be musicians before the Ark. Their job was to prophesy on those instruments. "Moreover David and the captains of the host separated to the service of the sons of Asaph, and of Heman, and of Jeduthun, who should *prophesy* with *harps*, with *psalteries*, and with *cymbals*..." (1 Chron. 25:1, emphasis mine).

These musicians did not only accompany the choir or congregational singing; they were part of the prophetic ministry in the church. They *prophesied* on their instruments. "Under the hands of their father Jeduthun, who prophesied with a *harp*, to give thanks and to praise the Lord" (1 Chron. 25:3b). The total number of musicians that David appointed to prophesy with instruments of music was 288.[1]

The Word of God mentions musical prophecy often. In the Book of First Samuel, the story is related how Samuel anointed Saul and kissed him, and then told Saul what was going to happen to him after he left:

> ...*As you approach the town, you will meet a procession of prophets coming down from the high place with* **lyres, tambourines, flutes** *and* **harps** *being played before them, and they will be prophesying. The Spirit of the Lord will come upon you in power, and you will prophesy with them; and you will be changed into a different person* (1 Samuel 10:5-6 NIV, emphasis mine).

---

1.   See 1 Chron. 25:7.

31

The Rebirth of Music

This group of prophets whom Saul met were playing instruments of music. These prophets used those musical instruments to worship the Lord. They then became inspired and prophesied. The worship and praise to God on the instruments invoked the presence of God. It also prepared the prophets' hearts to receive the word and prepared the hearts of the listeners to accept the word of the Lord.

Another prophet in the Old Testament requested that music be played before he prophesied:

> But now bring me a **minstrel**. And it came to pass, when the **minstrel** played, that the hand of the Lord came upon him [Elisha]. And he said, Thus saith the Lord... (2 Kings 3:15-16).

Elisha also knew the importance music has in invoking the presence of God. The minstrel played, and the music created an atmosphere of worship and praise in which God could dwell. God dwells in the praises of His people.[2] The ministry of music becomes even more powerful when God not only dwells in our music, but also through our music speaks a prophetic word.

It is my desire to see more Christian musicians flow in the prophetic. There are literally thousands of gospel music groups using music purely for evangelism. Praise the Lord for those who are hearing the gospel through music. But what about the millions of people who need to hear the prophetic word of God? What about those who need direction, comfort, and edification in their lives? God wants to use musicians as vessels through whom He can speak. The ministry of music is more than just reaching the unsaved. God wants musicians to prophesy on their instruments, to play a new song, a spontaneous song of praise and worship, completely unrehearsed. This requires musicians to be free in their worship, to allow the Holy Spirit to move upon them in an intuitive manner.

> Wherefore, brethren, covet to prophesy... (1 Corinthians 14:39).

---

2.   See Ps. 22:3.

Chapter Six

Music in War

Another spiritual purpose of music is war. On the surface this seems absurd, but think about the films you've seen of armies marching in perfect cadence to the martial sound of bugle and drum. Music will lift your emotions and spirit and, in turn, make your faith stronger. Perhaps that is why armies in history, even in the Bible, have gone to war singing.

Today God is gathering together an army who, empowered by the Holy Spirit, captained by Jesus Himself, will be a powerful force. God is commanding every soldier to "put on the whole armour of God, that ye may be able to stand against the wiles of the devil. For we wrestle not against flesh and blood, but against principalities, against powers, against the rulers of the darkness of this world, against spiritual wickedness in high places" (Eph. 6:11-12).

This army is the Church, His Bride, who is going to war against the enemy to drive back his influence. The army of the Lord is a musical army. It is an army who loves to sing and play instruments. God has commanded His people to, "let the high praises of God be in their mouth, and a two-edged sword in their hand" (Ps. 149:6).

God wants His army to be equipped not only with swords but also with praises. Note: These praises are not just ordinary praises (if praises can be ordinary), but these are "high praises"—praises that come out of our mouth with volume and with authority.

What is this army going to do with these swords and high praises? The Bible says they are going "to execute vengeance upon the heathen, and punishments upon the people; to bind their kings with chains, and their nobles with fetters of iron; to execute upon them the judgment written: this honour have all His saints..." (Ps. 149:7-9).

God is going to war with an army of worshipers—those who know how to praise loudly. Not that God needs us to fight for Him; He chooses to move through His body, the Church, in driving back the powers of darkness.

Musical War

Joshua commanded an army who knew how to sing, shout, and play instruments with volume. In Joshua 6, God was very specific about how He wanted this army to defeat the city of Jericho. Their one and only weapon was music and the shout of victory.

> Then the Lord said to Joshua, "...March around the city once with all the armed men. Do this for six days. Have seven priests carry **trumpets of rams' horns** in front of the ark. On the seventh day, march around the city seven times, with the priests blowing the **trumpets**. When you hear them sound a long blast on the **trumpets**, have all the people give a loud shout; then the wall of the city will collapse and the people will go up, every man straight in" (Joshua 6:2a-5 NIV, emphasis mine).

Joshua and his army did exactly what God commanded them to do. They picked up the Ark of the Covenant and put it on their shoulders. Seven priests positioned themselves in front of the Ark with trumpets in their hands. In front of the priests, as well as behind the Ark of the Covenant, went a company of armed guards.

When Joshua gave the order to advance, the mighty processional began. With the trumpets sounding, the army marched around the city. "The armed guard marched ahead of the priests who blew the *trumpets,* and the rear guard followed the ark. All this time the *trumpets* were sounding" (Josh. 6:9 NIV, emphasis mine).

Joshua led his army around the city of Jericho once each day for six days. On the seventh day, they did as God commanded Joshua and marched around the city seven times, all the while playing instruments. The Bible then says, "The seventh time around, when the priests sounded the *trumpet* blast, Joshua commanded the people, '*Shout*! For the Lord has given you the city!'...When the *trumpets* sounded, the people shouted, and at the sound of the *trumpet,* when the people gave a loud shout, the wall collapsed; so every man charged straight in, and they took the city" (Josh. 6:16,20 NIV, emphasis mine).

These Old Testament accounts are not just stories for our reading pleasure; they are for our instruction and example. God is instructing us, as a last-day generation, to prepare ourselves for confrontation with the enemy. He says nation will fight against nation and kingdom against kingdom. Then you will be handed over to be persecuted and put to death, and you shall be hated by every nation. But in the midst of this turmoil, God will still be in control and leading His army, and they will know no ultimate defeat. For in the midst of this army will be musicians playing instruments with authority and singers with high praises of God in their mouth. The entire host will march in strength and victory, rejoicing in their God. With the songs of worship resounding in volume, the gates of hell will not be able to stand against them. The walls will have to collapse at the shout of victory, for God is the Captain of this mighty host, and He dwells among them as they sing their praise.[1]

---

1. See Ps. 22:3.

A Song of Deliverance

There was another army in the Bible who also learned the secret of going to war with instruments of music. One day in the house of the Lord, as all of Judah was standing before the Lord asking for deliverance from the three armies that had come to destroy them, the Holy Spirit came upon one of the musicians. His name was Jahaziel, who was a fifth generation to Asaph, one of the chief musicians in David's tabernacle.

Jahaziel began to prophesy. "Listen, King Jehoshaphat and all who live in Judah and Jerusalem!...'Do not be afraid or discouraged because of this vast army. For the battle is not yours, but God's....You will not have to fight this battle....Go out to face them tomorrow, and the Lord will be with You' " (2 Chron. 20:15,17 NIV).

When all of Judah heard the word of God, they fell before the Lord and worshiped Him. Then they stood and praised the Lord with a loud voice.

In the morning, the people of Judah arose early and prepared themselves to go out and face the enemy. Jehoshaphat may or may not have known the secret and the power of the ministry of music in praise; nevertheless, he appointed singers "unto the Lord" (vs. 21). These singers were not the nation's superstars. They were not a club group recruited from the nearest Holiday Inn. They were singers who had a heart to worship God and lived a pure life before the Lord. They were appointed unto the Lord—not unto Jehoshaphat nor unto the people to entertain them—but unto the Lord to praise Him in the beauty of holiness.

The singers went out in front of the army. They were most likely a male choir; and the music probably had only one or two vocal parts.

*And when they began to **sing** and to praise, the Lord set ambushments against the children of Ammon, Moab, and mount Seir, which were come against Judah; and they were smitten* (2 Chronicles 20:22, emphasis mine).

The enemy, hearing the sound of their praises, had become frightened. The sound rolled across the landscape as claps of thunder. Judah was not even in view yet, but their music could be heard. When they started to sing and praise, the Lord set an ambush against the three armies who were out to destroy them.

There are many musicians who sing, but fewer who praise the Lord when they sing. The Bible doesn't say that when they sang and entertained the people, God set "ambushments" against the enemy. It says that when they praised, God's power was unleashed. This is the secret to the powerful ministry of music—the singers and musicians are appointed *unto the Lord* to *praise Him* in the beauty of holiness. God is challenging us as Christian musicians to be worshipers with our music, not just performers.

> *The men of Ammon and Moab rose up against the men from Mount Seir* [when they heard Judah's praises] *to destroy and annihilate them. After they finished slaughtering the men from Seir, they helped to destroy one another* (2 Chronicles 20:23 NIV).

I wonder whom the Lord used to ambush the enemy? Judah wasn't there yet. Do you suppose God sent a legion of angels to confuse the armies of Ammon, Moab, and Mount Seir? Some scholars say that these ambushments were invisible angels, whereas others believe that dissentions and fierce feuds broke out. Nevertheless, someone did the ambushing. Perhaps an angel picked up a sword and stabbed a man from Ammon through the heart. A friend of his saw it and thought the Moabite soldier standing nearby did it, and avenged his friend's death. And the rest is not difficult to imagine. No one saw the angels, while three armies were ambushed. Meanwhile the choir was still marching forward singing, "Praise the Lord for His mercy endureth forever and ever," not knowing what was happening on the other side of the hill.

> *When the men of Judah came to the place that overlooks the desert and looked toward the vast army, they saw only dead bodies lying on the ground; no one had escaped. So Jehoshaphat*

*and his men went to carry off their plunder, and they found among them a great amount of equipment and clothing and also articles of value—more than they could take away. There was so much plunder that it took three days to collect it. On the fourth day they assembled in the Valley of Beracah, where they praised the Lord. This is why it is called the Valley of Beracah to this day. Then, led by Jehoshaphat, all the men of Judah and Jerusalem returned joyfully to Jerusalem, for the Lord had given them cause to rejoice over their enemies. They entered Jerusalem and went to the temple of the Lord with **harps** and **lutes** and **trumpets*** (2 Chronicles 20:24-28 NIV, emphasis mine).

There are a lot of *secrets* in this story, teaching us many things. For example, these musicians and singers knew the secret of praising the Lord with their music in the valley and on the mountaintop. They worshiped on their instruments when surrounded by the enemy and when it seemed everything was against them. Likewise, when the victory came, they did not forget where it came from and returned to the temple to bless the Lord with their harps, lutes, and trumpets.

God is raising up strong and powerful ministries of music in churches around the world. He is preparing them to be leaders in warfare against the enemy. These worshiping singers and musicians will be going to battle against the enemy just as King Jehoshaphat did.

Chapter Seven

Music and Healing

Did you know that music can relieve nerve tension and restore a mind when it is fatigued? That it can bring joy and peace to a heart that is upset and troubled? That it can even reverse sickness and bring healing? Music, even in its natural state, can be used in a positive way to restore. If it can restore physical health, think of what it can do to restore our spiritual health when it is filled with the presence of God.

I have met several Christians who are trained music therapists. They use music to treat patients with various ailments. In fact, several state universities now offer courses in music therapy.

Music Medicine

The medical staff at the Veterans' Hospital in Lyons, New Jersey, conducted a project in music therapy and found it to be a great success in the treatment of nervous and mental disorders. Other hospitals have found music to be effective in the curing of arthritis and spastic-paralysis, and in the restoring of heart fatigue. Music relaxes and soothes people who are disturbed in their minds and tend to brood. It gives them some balance.

Amnesia can also be treated well through music. It can bring back forgotten memory associations more quickly than any other means. Patients are able to recall names, ideas, places, and people by listening to music. A song will trigger an idea, a color, a sound, or a picture; and those things that were lost in the past can be brought back to the patient's remembrance.

Music can free us from tension and lift our spirits when we are discouraged. It can literally move our emotions and then our will. Have you ever been upset and angry and determined to do something a certain way when you got home? As you were driving along, the music on the FM dial of the radio began to relax you. You began to rethink the situation, and before you arrived home, you changed your mind because you discovered your attitude had been too harsh.

Have you ever been driving in bumper-to-bumper traffic and noticed that your frustrations were either increasing or diminishing, depending on which radio station you were listening to? Obviously, there is an effect from the music that you listen to. Music can move your emotions, which, in turn, will move you. Music is a powerful tool.

Music is used in advertising to persuade you to think a certain product will change your life. Sociologists say that music is a vehicle for communicating, influencing, and controlling our spirit, mind, and body. A song will present a thought, and if you listen to that song enough times, it will reform your thought processes and then you will act differently. The vehicle of music is very commanding. It can be a powerful source for achieving positive or negative goals.

Mozart and Miracles

There have been historical accounts of healing through music in many cultures of the world.

- Eskimos of eastern Greenland settle their arguments with drums and a song, which they use to discharge their rage toward their enemy.

- In ancient Greece, Rome, and Egypt, the priests in the temples sang as they healed the afflicted.

- Young working mother, Vanessa, was healed of a tumor of the thymus gland by practicing visualizations, personal affirmations, and playing bowls that vibrated harmonious overtones.[1]

- Sufism, an Islamic sect, considers melodious sound as food for the soul, bringing health and peace.

- In World War II when musicians played for the wounded servicemen, they saw more results than just entertainment from the boredom of hospital life. Depressions lessened, expression increased, and contact with reality improved.[2]

Dr. Mitchell L. Gaynor, M.D., in his book *The Sounds of Healing*, states that the first evidence that music has healing potential involves the effects of music on a variety of physiologic functions and parameters. He discovered the following results:

- Reduced anxiety, heart rate, and respiratory rate: Forty patients who had suffered recent heart attacks were exposed to "relaxing music." Results indicated statistically significant reduction in anxiety, respiratory rate, and heart rate, which suggested to researchers that the use of music may be an effective way to reduce high levels of anxiety among heart patients.

- Reduced cardiac complications: The patients in the coronary care unit who suffered heart attacks had fewer complications when exposed to music for two days than those who were not exposed to it.

---

1. Mitchell L. Gaynor, *The Sounds of Healing* (Broadway, New York, NY 1999) 45-48.
2. *Sounds of Healing*, 78.

- Lowered blood pressure and heart rate: When listening to a variety of musical styles, both systolic and diastolic blood pressure may decrease by as much as five points per listening session. Heart rate may decrease by four to five beats per minute.

- Increased immune cell messengers: A 1993 report by scientists at Michigan State University disclosed that levels of interleukin-1 (an immune-cell messenger molecule that helps to regulate the activity of other immune cells) increased by 12.5 to 14 percent when subjects listened to music for 15-minute periods. Those who listened to Mozart or light jazz exhibited up to a 25 percent lower level of cortisol, a stress hormone that can depress the immune system when produced in excess. This led researchers to conclude that music of one's own choosing "may elicit a profound positive emotional experience that can trigger the release of hormones which can contribute to a lessening of those factors which enhance the disease process."

- Drop in stress hormones during medical testing.

- Boost in natural opiates: At the Addiction Research Center in Stanford, California, subjects listened to various kinds of music. Half of the subjects reported having a feeling of euphoria while listening, leading the researchers to suspect that the joy of music is mediated by the opiate chemicals known as endorphins—the brain's natural painkillers. They concluded that certain kinds of music boost endorphins, which have other health benefits, including a stronger immune system.

Is There a Musician in the House?

When King Saul was bothered by an evil spirit, he probably received very bad headaches and became physically and mentally sick. There were times when Saul became very depressed and afraid.

But the Spirit of the Lord departed from Saul, and an evil spirit from the Lord troubled him. And Saul's servants said unto *him, Behold now, an evil spirit from God troubleth thee. Let our lord now command thy servants, which are before thee, to seek out a man, who is a **cunning player** on an **harp**: and it shall come to pass, when the evil spirit from God is upon thee, that he shall **play** with his hand, and thou shalt be well* (1 Samuel 16:14-16, emphasis mine).

Somehow, King Saul's servants knew about the powerful remedy of music. Perhaps they knew from past experience, or perhaps that knowledge had been passed down to them from generation to generation.

Notice it was not good enough for the servants to call just any harp player. The suggestion to the king by the servants was to look hard for a cunning or very skillful player. "And Saul said unto his servants, Provide me now a man that can *play* well, and bring him to me" (1 Sam. 16:17, emphasis mine).

One of the servants spoke up and informed King Saul that he had seen one of the sons of Jesse, the Bethlehemite, who was not only a very talented musician, but good-looking, brave, and strong, with a good head on his shoulders. Everyone knew that the Lord was with David. Saul took the suggestion from his servant and sent a messenger to bring this lad to him.

Jesse was pleased that the king wanted to see his son, so he sent David with an ass loaded with bread, wine, and a young goat. When Saul saw David, he immediately liked him and asked David to be his armorbearer and bodyguard. David was always near Saul so that when the evil spirit bothered Saul, David could play his harp and the music would soothe the king.

*And it came to pass, when the evil spirit from God was upon Saul, that David took **an harp**, and **played** with his hand: so Saul was refreshed, and was well, and the evil spirit departed from him* (1 Samuel 16:23, emphasis mine).

Note here that it was purely on the presentation of a song of worship by a skillful musician that Saul was delivered from the evil spirit. No doctor treated him. It was not a tranquilizer that subdued the disturbing influence of the evil spirit. It was the delivering power of the presence of God that set Saul free. Perhaps David didn't sing a word—just "played with his hand." The anointing of the Lord's presence on a worshiper's music broke the bands that had King Saul tied to the evil spirit.

> *And it shall come to pass in that day, that his burden shall be taken away from off thy shoulder, and his yoke from off thy neck, and the yoke shall be destroyed because of the anointing* (Isaiah 10:27).

This is probably the first written account in history of music therapy. However, please note that the difference between natural music therapy and spiritual music therapy is the presence of God the healer in the music. Therefore, it must be the music David played—worship.

Music Malady

Music is good medicine, and it can bring healing; however, at the same time it can bring sickness, depending upon what form we listen to. Performers of loud music can suffer from ulcers, insomnia, and heart trouble. Due to increased volume, certain types of music can bring intense pain to the body of the performer and to the audience. Music always affects the body. It is a powerful instrument. Music can hypnotize; it can put you to sleep; it can make you hyper.

It has been proven that certain sound waves, low enough in frequency, can even kill you. These waves lie in the range below your hearing (infasonics). Even at seven cycles per second, sound can cause considerable pain and has the potential to kill people, en masse, up to five miles away. Music can be a tremendous destructive force or a tremendous healing force.

God commanded us to *sing* praises to Him in the *beauty* of holiness. He knew those harmonious notes would bring health to His people. Let us as musicians and singers be responsible with our music and minister to people in healing. Let us bring peace and deliverance through music played in the name of the Lord.

44

Chapter Eight

Music and Exorcism

The crescendo of the music was intense. People lifted their voices to a higher level and with great passion. Suddenly, two women got down on their hands and knees and began to walk on all fours, purring like cats. This was an unusual sight in the middle of a Christian worship service. We continued singing our worship spontaneously to God. The scene became even more intense. One woman began to hiss aggressively. Others came forward and spoke to the woman in the name of Jesus.

I did not have much experience with spirits, but it looked as though there was another force present. We had company. The woman was controlled by evil spirits. Demons often hide below the surface of a person's personality and are not always evident. But when we sing the praise in which God dwells, they are often challenged to the surface and manifest on the face or in the behavior of the person they possess.

Exorcism With a Guitar

So it came about whenever the evil spirit from God came to Saul, David would take the harp and play it with his hand; and Saul would be refreshed and be well, and the evil spirit would depart from him (1 Samuel 16:23 NAS).

In this account of David exorcising the demon troubling Saul, he used music. I believe that David was not ministering to Saul on the natural level only, for indeed music has a healing and soothing quality to it as we discovered in the previous chapter. There had to be something powerful enough spiritually to force the displacement of the evil spirit. Demons often like to hold on and have to be forced out of their hiding place where they can control at will.

The phrase "evil spirit from God," in the Scripture above, actually means "by the permission of God." Some say that it means "an evil spirit from before the Lord." Nevertheless, God allowed or permitted this spirit to trouble and terrify Saul. He grew fretful, discontented, and suspicious by the influence of the evil spirit. He would tremble at times and appear to be choking or strangled, typical of demonic fits. The presence of the evil spirit lets us know this was not a natural disease. Many scholars do not know how to interpret this incident.

The remedy was to seek a man who was a skillful player on the harp.[1] Note the emphasis on a *skillful* player. This was someone who was knowledgeable about the harp and could play well. One of the king's servants recommended David to Saul. He was of very high character, a man of courage and good conduct, prudent in all matters. The crowning and most significant point was that "the Lord [was] with him" (1 Sam. 16:18b). David ministered to the Lord in musical worship, most probably with his harp. It is evident in his psalms and historic chronicles that he was a worshiper. That is why the Lord's presence was with him. He was not just favored of the Lord, but rather, the presence of God was on his life and heart.

---

1.   See 1 Sam. 16:16.

I am convinced that a key to signs and wonders by means of musical praise is the character and purity of the musician, as well as the pure and powerful presence of God. Concerts and perform-ance (acting and pretense) in the name of worship are not power-ful in the supernatural realm; they are only an artistic expression. David was a man of character and purity of heart (even though he made some serious mistakes) and he had a passion for the pres-ence of God. Some musicians have only a passion to play music.

The secret lies with the heart of David. He was a worshiper. He worshiped as a child and continued, as he matured, to express passion for the presence of God. Worship invokes the presence of God. When David played, it wasn't only testimony songs, specials, or cover tunes. He played worship to God. So the key to this exor-cism was David's "mode of operation"—he worshiped whenever he could. He was a God-chaser who wanted to spend time in the pres-ence of God more than he wanted to live in the palace.[2]

The harp David used to express his worship was a lyre—a small, light portable stringed instrument in the shape of a bow. It could be played sitting down or standing. (For references as to where this instrument is mentioned in the Scriptures, see the Appendix.)

Musicians Expel Demons

I distinctly remember the power of praise over evil spirits as I was holding a worship seminar in North Pole, Alaska. When I was setting up the equipment for the opening service, a young Native American boy followed me around. I tried to make conversation with him, but he wouldn't respond. I became a little concerned, but then I got busy and forgot about him.

Later that evening, I was leading worship, and we had just fin-ished singing a familiar song and began to sing spontaneously our own personal song. There was a real sense of God's presence. I heard a commotion to my left, and there on the front row was this

---

2.   See Ps. 27:4.

boy, writhing in unusual contortions. His grandfather, a medicine man, had "blessed" him, which in actuality was a curse. Demons were trying to interrupt the worship and bring attention to themselves. As we continued to worship and the dark spirit was forced to leave, the boy was fine.

There have been instances like this in other parts of the world—Mexico, Greece, and Argentina where I have used the guitar to do exorcisms. I followed the pattern that David used in freeing Saul of evil spirits. I believe he worshiped with his fingers and God's presence came. David might have sung, but there is no record of him doing so. God rules as King and Judge in the place where we praise Him.

Chapter Nine

Which Music Is of God?

There has been much controversy throughout church history about which music is appropriate for Christians to listen to and which instruments should be permitted in church services. When I was 14 years of age and learning to play the guitar, a church in the town where I lived had a difficult time accepting the guitar as an instrument that could be played in the Christian worship. After a while, the leadership of this church realized that guitars were popular with the young people. So, in their youth meetings, they allowed acoustic guitars to be played in the sanctuary, but still no electric guitars and amplifiers were allowed in the church services.

It is interesting to note that today, in many of those same churches, you will find amplifiers on the platform—not only amplifiers, but drums as well. Did God change His mind? Was it once wrong to use certain instruments in church in our worship but now it is okay? Or did man create those restrictions?

Which Musical Instruments Does God Allow Us to Use?

I think the answer is quite obvious. God commanded His people thousands and thousands of years ago to:

*Praise the Lord with the **harp**; make music to Him on the **ten-stringed lyre**. Sing to Him a new song; **play** skillfully, and shout for joy* (Psalm 33:2-3 NIV, emphasis mine).

*Sing for joy to God our strength; shout aloud to the God of Jacob! Begin the **music**, strike the **tambourine**, play the melodious **harp** and **lyre**. Sound the **ram's horn** [trumpet] at the New Moon...* (Psalm 81:1-3 NIV, emphasis mine).

*And of Zion it shall be said....As well the singers as the **players** on **instruments** shall be there...* (Psalm 87:5-7, emphasis mine).

It is clear that God has ordained in Zion, His Church, musical instruments as well as singers to blend together to worship His name. Even today there are some people who find it hard to accept certain instruments used to worship God. God is doing a whole new thing in the ministry of music in His Church. Churches all over the world are using all kinds of instruments, including native instruments, to worship the Lord. And these churches are discovering that the joy of expressive worship can be found in God's house. They are finding liberty in their worship.

Man has said, "Guitars and drums are of the devil," but God has said that we are to:

*Praise Him with the sound of the **trumpet**: praise Him with the **psaltery** and **harp**. Praise Him with the **timbrel** [tambourine] and dance: praise Him with **stringed instruments** and **organs**. Praise Him upon the **loud cymbals**: praise Him upon the high sounding **cymbals*** (Psalm 150:3-5, emphasis mine).

These are all instruments known in David's time. But just to make sure that we don't exclude any other instruments in our worship, the Bible says,

*Meanwhile, David and all the house of Israel were celebrating before the Lord with **all kinds** of instruments made of fir wood, and with lyres, harps, tambourines, castanets and cymbals* (2 Samuel 6:5 NAS, emphasis mine).

God does not want us to get hung up on types of instruments. The important thing is that we praise Him. That is why Psalm 150 ends with a command of the Lord: *"Praise ye the Lord."*

David instituted the use of musical instruments in worship as a pioneer of a worship reformation.

Four thousand [were] *gatekeepers, and 4,000* [were] *praising the Lord with the instruments which David made for giving praise* (1 Chronicles 23:5 NAS).

*With them Heman and Jeduthun, to sound aloud with trumpets and cymbals and the musical **instruments of God**. Now the sons of Jeduthun were gatekeepers* (1 Chronicles 16:42 NKJ, emphasis mine).

These instruments were created by man and dedicated to the service of worship of Yahweh. As a result, these instruments were called the "instruments of God." In like manner, you could lay your hands on your guitar or keyboard and dedicate it to God, calling it a "musical instrument of God," provided you use it only for the worship of Him.

If we love Him, we will praise Him the way He wants us to. It's a command. We don't do it just because we feel like it, but because God commands His people to praise Him. If He wishes that we praise Him with all kinds of musical instruments, then we should. Let everything praise the Lord.

Which Music Is Okay?

Not only has there been much controversy about which types of instruments have a place in the church, but there has also been much discussion over certain styles of music. Do certain types of music have a place in the Body of Christ? Which music should Christians listen to?

The Rebirth of Music

All music originally came from God. It was God who created the tambourines, pipes, and viols in lucifer in the first place. Man was not on the scene yet, and there possibly were no musical instruments prior to that. It was God who inspired David to invent and make instruments. God seemed to confirm the use of them with His manifest presence as they were played.[1] Because God gave man the creativity to invent and make instruments, can they not all be used in worship of Him?

> *And David spake to the chief of the Levites to appoint their brethren to be the singers with instruments of music, psalteries and harps and cymbals, sounding, by lifting up the voice with joy....So David, and the elders of Israel, and the captains over thousands, went to bring up the ark of the covenant of the Lord out of the house of Obededom with joy. And it came to pass, when* **God helped** *the Levites that bare the ark of the covenant of the Lord, that they offered seven bullocks and seven rams* (1 Chronicles 15:16,25-26, emphasis mine).

However, I've noticed that the closer musicians get to being like the world, the more flesh, sensuality, pride, and darkness can be seen in them and their presentations, rather than the sincere Spirit of God. Christian groups who idolize secular music and try to copy other groups in the world, place themselves in a very compromising situation. There is a different spirit by which that music was created and is played. It has a different purpose, possibly to appeal to the sex drive in teenagers, to pull emotional strings, or to incite a negative reaction from its listeners.

We aren't to be so much like the world that the world can't see any difference in us. If we act like the world and have a spirit like those who do not know Christ, we are not pleasing Jesus. Rather, we are to be "set apart from the world." "If you were of the world, the world would love its own; but because you are not of

---

1.   See 2 Chron. 5:13.

the world, but I chose you out of the world, therefore the world hates you" (Jn. 15:19 RSV).

The word *world* in this Scripture refers to the "kosmos." The best definition of it is "1) the ungodly multitude; the whole mass of men alienated from God, and therefore hostile to the cause of Christ or the 2) world affairs, the aggregate of things earthly, the whole circle of earthly goods, endowments, riches, advantages, pleasures, etc., which although hollow and frail and fleeting, stir desire, seduce from God, and are obstacles to the cause of Christ."[2]

We are not to be "of the earthly goods that are obstacles to the cause of Christ" but separate from this "world." We are to keep ourselves unstained from this kind of spirit and system.[3] "...Do you not know that friendship with the world is enmity with God? Whoever therefore wants to be a friend of the world makes himself an enemy of God" (Jas. 4:4 NKJ).

God has enlarged our vision. He wants us to offer more to people than just a few fancy guitar licks and some funky piano solos. God wants us to offer salvation, the truths of the Holy Spirit and His presence. God wants us to share these with others, not only by our words, but through our music as well. We are to let people see Jesus in us. If they can't see Jesus, then there is too much flesh—too much of us. We must decrease, and God must increase.

Because God is enlarging the spectrum of Christian music available today, there is no need to copy secular music. Let us, as Christian musicians, be creative to invent or produce new instrumentation and sounds. Our heavenly Father is *the Creator;* can we not be *the creative* force in the earth? The deck is definitely stacked in the Christian's favor in the area of creativity. Some Christian musicians are so obsessed with tracking what is "hot" or current on the billboard charts that they erroneously copy the performance of

2. *Thayer's Bible Dictionary* (public domain).
3. See Jas. 1:27.

secular musicians. Yes, God also created secular musicians in the image of Himself and gave them creativity as well. But they do not possess the spirit of worship or the Spirit of God. If you take lessons from someone who is not a Christian to learn a technique, just beware not to drink of his or her spirit.

Songs of the World

There is a difference between the "song of the Lord" and the "song of the world." Songs *of* God and *for* God are of a different kingdom, philosophy, and spirit. Songs of the world fit into one of three categories: the world, the flesh, or the devil.

Songs of the *world* may be just pretty love songs about a wife, a puppy, or a gorgeous sunset. There is nothing necessarily wrong with these songs; they may be beautiful and express love and admiration for a person or object on a natural level.

Songs of the *flesh* are generally lusty songs that are sensual and dirty. They are sexual; the thoughts of these songs present ideas that appeal to us sexually. They are smutty and serve only to edify the flesh. These songs fulfill the lust of the flesh and the lust of the eyes. They have the spirit of the pride of life—arrogant, in your face, and self-centered.

Songs of the *devil* are songs of the kingdom of satan. These songs are dark and evil. They present thoughts of blasphemy, and exalt lucifer or satan as the supreme being. They are dark and have evidence of a desire to steal, destroy, or kill the listener. Songs that glorify suicide, for example, entice the listeners to kill themselves. Without Christ, they go to hell—satan the ultimate terrorist, permanently captures another hostage.

For all that is in the world—the lust of the flesh, the lust of the eyes, and the pride of life—is not of the Father but is of the world. And the world is passing away, and the lust of it; but he who does the will of God abides forever (1 John 2:16-17 NKJ).

There are many songs that fit into these three categories. It is surprising how many Christians won't watch a smutty scene on television or go to a restricted movie, but will listen continually to music of the flesh or devil. Without realizing it, they are feeding their minds with dirty and suggestive thoughts, and satisfying their flesh. The Bible says we are to crucify the deeds of the flesh. The more we listen to music that talks about getting high on dope or about leaving your wife for another woman, the more we are feeding our minds with thoughts that are directly in conflict with God's Word and our spiritual and natural health.

Lyrics of many of today's songs advocate quick sensual gratification, not just sexuality, but all sorts of "feel goods." But God teaches us to do what is right, not what feels good. Are we listening to the world's music more than we are listening to positive music that feeds our spirit with a healthy diet? If there is any doubt, stay away from it. Yet as Christians, we continue to feed our minds with this garbage that is full of lust and greed, and then wonder why we have such a struggle serving the Lord.

"For as he thinks in his heart, so is he..." (Prov. 23:7 NKJ).

Songs of the Lord

As Christians we should be feeding our minds with wholesome songs—songs of victory and faith, songs of power, songs of love, and songs of grace, joy, and peace. The Bible says, "...whatsoever things are true, whatsoever things are honest, whatsoever things are just, whatsoever things are pure, whatsoever things are lovely, whatsoever things are of good report; if there be any virtue, and if there be any praise, think on these things" (Phil. 4:8).

We should not feed ourselves with the garbage of the world but with things that are pure, things that are honest, things that are true, things that are just, and things that are lovely and of good report. These things are what we're to think about. These things are what we're to sing about. These things are what we're to listen to.

Look what happens when you remove the word *things* and substitute the word *songs* in this verse: Whatsoever songs are true, whatsoever songs are honest, whatsoever songs are just, whatsoever songs are pure, whatsoever songs are lovely, whatsoever songs are of good report; if there be any virtue, and if there be any praise, sing these songs (or think on these songs)!

Today, the Church has access to music of excellence that exalts and magnifies the Lord and that is appealing to many different tastes. We don't need to compromise our morality to listen to quality music. Our Father in not the devil, but our Father which is in Heaven. Let's remember who our Father is and serve Him with songs that exalt the Lord and edify the believer and not serve the kingdom of darkness.

The Power of Music

Sociologists in secular circles have proven that music is extremely powerful. First, it communicates an idea or thought. Then it influences our view of that idea. Finally, it controls our mind, soul, and spirit. Think of the negative power that is available to lucifer and what he can do with music. Then consider the positive potential music can have in building up the Body of Jesus Christ and the Kingdom of God.

If music of the world can program our minds, then what kind of music we listen to is a very serious consideration. There may be nothing wrong with a song about love between a girl and boy, but songs that are dirty and magnify lucifer have no place in the life of a born-again Christian or the life of anyone for that matter because of its harmful potential. God wants there to be a definite line drawn in our music. He wants us to clean up our act.

Love Not the World—Nor Its Music

The Bible says: "Let the word of Christ dwell in you richly in all wisdom" (Col. 3:16a). Are you into the Word as much as you are into your music? We are to teach the Word to others through "psalms and hymns and spiritual songs, singing with grace in your hearts to the Lord" (Col. 3:16b).

Musicians are called to be priests or teachers of the Word; therefore, our songs should have biblical and moral content. A song with scriptural content is music that is "of" God and "from" God. Christian musician, do you love the music of the world? Why!? God says, "If any man love the world, the love of the Father is not in *him*." Those are heavy words. He wants us to play songs that are wholesome, that are clean, that edify the believer or exalt Jesus as Lord—those songs that clearly show Jesus to the world.

The world does not see Jesus in those songs that have a double meaning, that can be taken either way. When people hear a song about love that has no mention of God, they do not automatically think about Jesus. They will not assume you are singing about God even if they know you are a Christian.

What Makes the Song Bad?

There are three ways to judge music for healthy content. First review the lyrics. Is there something obviously vulgar, violent, or unhealthy for the listener? Lyrics reveal the spirit and purpose of the song. Sometimes there are double meanings that a subculture or another generation will know about but someone in the mainstream will not recognize. So ask the question, "What does this mean?" Teenagers may argue that lyrics aren't important because they don't listen to the words. However, inquire to know and understand the meaning of the song. Going through this process trains children how to discern and judge music.

The second way to judge a song is by the music. This method is more subjective, with personal tastes getting in the way. Some people say music is of the devil because it is loud. Others say certain beats are of the devil. Neither statement is true. There is no mention in Scripture of certain rhythms being evil. On the contrary, the Bible says to bring forth the beat.[4] There is nothing

---

4.   See Ps. 81:1-2—"bring hither the timbrel" (percussion or beat).

essentially dark or evil about certain beats or chords. There is no mention in Scripture of any musical style or certain musical parts that are not of God.

The third way to discern music is by its spirit. This is also subjective according to the intuitive ability of the listener. However, the composer, arranger, and performer all have a part in the spirit, and there is something imparted from the song, music, and lyrics to the listener. Those who write and perform the song have the greatest involvement in flavoring the spirit of the music, which can include darkness, anger, violence, and hatred. The song can be sexual, lustful, and sensual, exhibiting a spirit of lust. These types of spirits will negatively impact the listener.

When discerning the positive or negative qualities of music, try to detach your tastes in music. It is the lyrics and spirit of the music that will give you the best insight. Music of itself is not wrong. It is the spirit in the music that flavors it.

Remember, God wants us to sing and play music that will exalt Jesus as Lord, songs that are pure and that will edify the believer. Which music is of God? Which music is of the world? It should be very clear if you ask the question, "Who, or what, does it exalt?" Is the answer, "The world, the flesh, or the devil"? Music of God has musical lyrics that exalt Jesus and/or edify the believer. Think on the things that are pure, and listen to that music which is wholesome, and you will be a happier, more victorious Christian.

In his book *Music Through the Eyes of Faith*, Hart Best says,

"Let's concentrate on something that almost never comes to mind: The music that Jesus heard and made throughout His life—the music of the wedding feast, the dance, the street, and the synagogue. As it turns out, Jesus was not a composer but a carpenter. Thus, He heard and used the music made by other, fallen creatures—the very ones He died to redeem.

"The ramifications of this single fact are enormous! They assist in answering the questions as to whether music used by Christians can only be written by Christians and whether music written by non-Christians is somehow non-Christian. But for now, it is important to understand that even though we don't know whether every piece of music Jesus used was written by people of faith, we can be sure that it was written by imperfect people, bound by the conditions of a fallen world and hampered by sinfulness and limitation."[5]

How Does God Like His Music?

In more than one thousand Scriptures regarding music, I have never read that God wants music played softly. He may like it that way, but we are never instructed in Scripture to play "pianissimo." God likes music loud.[6]

*So the children of Israel who were present at Jerusalem kept the Feast of Unleavened Bread seven days with great gladness; and the Levites and the priests praised the Lord day by day, singing to the Lord, accompanied by **loud instruments** (2 Chronicles 30:21 NKJ, emphasis mine).*

The worship of the Lord in the Scriptures was often with loud music. Keep in mind that they did not have electronic amplification, so I am not advocating playing so loud that our ears hurt. But the principle is to play out unto the Lord and make His praise *great*. For we are to praise Him equally to His excellent greatness.[7] He is not your average God. He is *the God* among the gods, so the praise of Him should be *the praise* among the gods.

"Praise Him upon the *loud* cymbals: praise Him upon the high sounding cymbals" (Ps. 150:5, emphasis mine). The word *high* means to split the ears with sound like a clangor of trumpets. We should give Him our utmost for His highest. The principle is to proclaim His greatness by lifting up the voice and instrument.

5.   Harold M. Best, *Music Through the Eyes of Faith* (Harper Collins: 1993), 18-19.
6.   See Ex. 19:16; 2 Chron. 15:14; 20:19; 30:21; Neh. 9:4.
7.   See Ps. 150:2.

The Rebirth of Music

"Sing unto Him a new song; play skillfully with a *loud* noise" (Ps. 33:3, emphasis mine). Play skillfully with a blast, shout, or noisy acclamation.

God also likes music that comes from our heart, spontaneous and sincere. Performed music, practiced and played from memory, is not His favorite. For He likes the new songs we sing that are personal and original.[8] He especially delights in those songs when we sing them for the first time.

God likes those songs that are sung to Him and sung from the heart. Encouraging the Ephesian church to attain the proper focus in their worship music, Paul writes, "[Speak] to yourselves in psalms and hymns and spiritual songs, singing and making melody in your heart to the Lord" (Eph. 5:19). These are the aspects to consider when contemplating what music God likes and what music we should play and listen to.

---

8.   See Ps. 22:3 (*tehillah* is the new song and God chooses to inhabit it); Ps. 40:3.

Chapter Ten

Music, Restoration, and Revival

Music formed an essential part of the national worship of Yahweh, and elaborate arrangements were made for its correct and extravagant presentation. These are detailed in First Chronicles where we are told that the whole body of the temple chorus and orchestra numbered 4,000, that they were trained and conducted in 24 divisions by the sons of Asaph, Heman, and Jeduthun. In each group, experts and novices were combined, so that the experts preserved the correct tradition, and the novices were trained to take their place. When worship waned, this tradition was lost.

Every reformation of faith brought with it a reconstruction of the temple chorus and orchestra, and a resumption of their duties. Thus when Hezekiah purged the state and church of the heathenism patronized by Ahaz, "He set the Levites in the house of [Yahweh] with cymbals, with psalteries, and with harps" (2 Chron. 29:25a). The same thing took place under Josiah.[1] After the

---

1.   See 2 Chron. 34.

restoration, at the dedication of the Temple[2] and at the dedication of the walls of Jerusalem,[3] music played a great part. In Nehemiah's time, the descendants of the ancient choral guilds drew together, and their maintenance was secured to them out of the public funds in return for their services.[4]

Joy-filled music in the Church has always been a sign of restoration and revival. Restoration is the bringing back or reestablishing of something as it once was. This is also what revival is—reviving or returning to a former state. What was dying will be made alive again. What was lost shall be found. Revival is not a week of meetings—it is a rebirth.

Revival Music

Music has always been associated with revival. In Church history, with every restoration of doctrinal truth, there has been a restoration in the ministry of music. With every new revelation of Scripture, there has been a fresh revelation in the music in the Church. Why? Music is an outward response of an inward rebirth.

The Reformation period clearly bears this out. With the increase in the knowledge and revelation of God's Word, there came forth a new song. Previously, during the Dark Ages, there was little music in the Church; only those in the religious hierarchy were allowed to chant their prayers. In the fourth century, the Council of the Laodecia banned the singing of the laity, which meant that common people were not allowed to sing in the Church. Only clergy could sing, and then only prescribed chants and prayers. For almost one thousand years, believers did not sing in public worship.

When Martin Luther received the revelation of the meaning of the Scripture, "The just shall live by faith" (Rom. 1:17b), there sprang up a spiritual rebirth in the Church. The printing press

---

2.   See Ezra 3:10.
3.   See Neh. 12:27.
4.   *International Standard Bible Encyclopaedia*, Electronic Database (Biblesoft, 1996).

made it possible for Bibles to be mass-produced in many languages. Believers were able to read God's Word for themselves, and this fueled a spiritual renewal. In the revival that followed, there came out of the Church a new sound. The Church began to sing songs again for the first time since the early Church. Luther wrote songs that were contemporary with the latest chords and rhythms, songs that even the common people could sing in worship to God.

And so it was with every truth that was restored to the Church, there was a restoration in music. Even at the turn of the century when the Holy Spirit was poured out in California, there was a new sound in the Church. People began to sing praises. There was a rebirth in the ministry of music as well.

Then in the early 1950s, with the restoration of the truth of the fivefold ministries—apostle, prophet, evangelist, pastor, and teacher—and the restoration of the laying on of hands, there was once again new music in the Church. Christians began to sing Scripture songs and songs in the Spirit as well.

In the 1960s, a new sound of worship came out of the Jesus People Renewal. Then, again in the 1990s, new sounds of worship sprang up in local churches in the U.S., Australia, and England, bringing to popularity many new songwriters, worship leaders, and movements. There was a renewal that touched the heart, and musicians chronicled it in song as their hearts sang.

The Lord has also restored other types of music to the Church: psalms, hymns, and spiritual songs. *Psalms* is translated from the Hebrew (*tehillum*) meaning "praises." In the Hebrew it is also *zamar*, which is to sing praise, make music, and play a stringed instrument. Another Hebrew word translated "psalms" is *zamiyr*,[5] meaning a song accompanied with musical instruments. In the New Testament the Greek word for "psalms" is *psalmos*,[6] which means to strike or twang. The reference, I believe, is to a stringed

---

5.   James Strong, *Strong's Exhaustive Concordance of the Bible* (Peabody, MA: Hendrickson Publishers, n.d.) **zamiyr** (#2158).

6.   *Strong's*, **psalmos** (#5568).

instrument. So when you read the word *psalms* in the New Testament, it almost always means singing or music with the use of stringed instruments. Yes, musical instruments were used in the New Testament. Paul encouraged the churches in Corinth and Ephesus to use instruments in Holy Spirit music.[7]

In the Bible, *hymns* were sacred songs sung to a Diety. Hymns mentioned in the New Testament are not hymns in a hymnbook as we know them today, because that form of music never existed until fourteen hundred years later. There are no Scriptures to defend the use of the style of music called "hymns." This word in the Bible did not refer to a *style of music*, but rather a *mode of music*.

Spiritual songs were songs received, sung, and quickened by the Holy Spirit. They were an instantaneous, spontaneous, or extemporaneous song. They were personal and the creation of the individual worship inspired by the Holy Spirit.

Ancient Worship Reformations

In the Old Testament there were many revivals of truth in which music was a part. In the revival under Nehemiah, music was present. One of the first things that Nehemiah did after the city of Jerusalem was rebuilt was appoint singers.

> *Now it came to pass, when the wall was built, and I had set up the doors, and the porters and the* **singers**...*were appointed* (Nehemiah 7:1, emphasis mine).

Nehemiah knew the importance of music, that it was an integral part of the restoration of worship. Nehemiah was aware of the place that music had in the lives of God's people, so he appointed singers. He chose them and set them in their place.

> *The whole congregation together was forty and two thousand three hundred and threescore, besides their manservants and their maidservants, of whom there were seven thousand three*

---

7. See 1 Cor. 14:15; Eph. 5:19; Col. 3:16.

*hundred thirty and seven: and they had two hundred forty and five **singing men** and **singing women*** (Nehemiah 7:66-67, emphasis mine).

*Of the sons of Asaph, the **singers** were over the business of the house of God. For it was the king's commandment concerning them, that a certain portion should be for the **singers**, due for every day* (Nehemiah 11:22b-23, emphasis mine).

The singers were part of the worship ministry of the Church and were paid by the tithes of the congregation.[8] They devoted much of their time to worshiping God, and to writing, playing, and ministering in music. They probably spent time arranging, practicing, and directing music for the temple worship.

There was another revival in Judah when Priest Jehoiada restored the ministry of worship in the house of the Lord. He also knew the importance of music in the Church and appointed the offices of musicians and singers.

*Also Jehoiada appointed the offices of the house of the Lord by the hand of the priests the Levites, whom David had distributed in the house of the Lord, to offer the burnt offerings of the Lord, as it is written in the law of Moses, with rejoicing and with **singing**, as it was ordained by David* (2 Chronicles 23:18, emphasis mine).

Jehoiada was careful to set up the worship just the way God commanded it to be in the Law of Moses, and ordained it by David in his tabernacle. It was getting *back* to the Word of God, *back* to the truth that had been lost.

Notice that when Israel fell into idolatry and carnality, the first thing to go was the ministry of music. And the first thing to come when we lose out spiritually is depression and the loss of joy. The prophetic songs of God can no longer flow out of a people. When this happens, the anointing and presence of God disappear. One

---

8.   See Neh. 13:5.

incident in the history of Israel showing this very clearly is what happened when the children of Israel grew bored and restless waiting for Moses to return from Mount Sinai. Together they asked Aaron to make a god for them, because they thought their God had left them. They gathered all the gold and jewelry together, made a golden calf, and began to worship their idol. When Moses came down from the mountain with two tables of stone, he found the people dancing and singing around the calf of gold.

> *And when Joshua heard the noise of the people as they shouted,*
> *he said unto Moses, There is a noise of war in the camp. And*
> *he said, It is...the noise of them that **sing** do I hear* (Exodus
> 32:17-18, emphasis mine).

The music they were singing and the songs they were playing were so chaotic and confusing that it sounded to Joshua like the torment and horror of war. Joshua never knew the music of Egypt, which is a type of the world or flesh, but Moses did. Joshua did not recognize the music Israel was making, but Moses, having come from Egypt, did. One of the very first things Israel lost when they fell into idolatry was the anointed ministry of music and the peace and harmony it brings.

Music Is Important to God

Under Hezekiah, when God moved again in Israel, one of the first things to be restored was the song of the Lord and the anointing on the music. Hezekiah appointed the singers and the musicians just as Nehemiah did:

> *And he* [Hezekiah] *set the Levites in the house of the Lord with*
> ***cymbals**, with **psalteries**, and with **harps**, according to the com-*
> *mandment of David, and of Gad the king's seer, and Nathan*
> *the prophet: for so was the commandment of the Lord by his*
> *prophets* (2 Chronicles 29:25, emphasis mine).

This Scripture clearly points out that God has commanded, through His prophets, that music be a ministry in worship and be set up according to His pattern, which is found in the tabernacle of David.

> *And the Levites stood with the **instruments** of David, and the priests with the **trumpets**. And Hezekiah commanded to offer the burnt offering upon the altar. And when the burnt offering began, the **song of the Lord** began also with the **trumpets**, and with the **instruments** ordained by David king of Israel. And all the congregation worshiped, and the **singers sang**, and the **trumpeters sounded*** (2 Chronicles 29:26-28a, emphasis mine).

Hezekiah, like David, had a heart for worship. He knew the Law of Moses, the commandments of David, and the prophecies of Nathan the prophet. He knew how to set God's house in order. That is what is called revival. Music is an evidence of a rebirth in God's people. When they receive again a revelation of truth, they will experience again a joyous sound. You show me a church that loves to sing, and I'll show you a church that is spiritually alive. You show me a person who can't find it within himself to sing and rejoice, and I'll show you someone who has nothing to sing about. You show me a worship musician who is bubbling over with joyful music, and I'll show you a musician who has a fresh revelation of Jesus.

Chapter Eleven

Music in Heaven

One of the most exciting revelations that came to me personally was when I discovered, for the first time, that there will be music in Heaven. When I was a young boy, I had heard that when we, as born-again Christians, die, we are translated into Heaven, each one of us having wings and white robes. I had imagined that our activities in Heaven would consist of flying around from cloud to cloud, playing a harp and trying to keep out of mischief. However, I soon learned that this was not true.

Through reading and studying the Scriptures regarding music, I discovered that the redeemed of the Lord will wear white robes and will be involved in musical worship to God. John saw this very clearly when God gave him a vision of Heaven.

The Singers

After these things I looked, and behold, a great multitude which no one could number, of all nations, tribes, peoples, and tongues, standing before the throne and before the Lamb, clothed with white robes, with palm branches in their hands, and crying out with a loud voice, saying, "Salvation belongs to our God who sits on the throne, and to the Lamb!" (Revelation 7:9-10 NKJ).

This multitude was from every race and culture in the world who have accepted God's free gift of salvation. God allowed John to see them in white robes signifying the righteousness they will have received through Jesus Christ.

But John not only saw them, he also heard them singing with a loud voice while waving palms in their hands. We will actually be waving palms, as Israel did when Jesus rode into Jerusalem on a colt. Instead of throwing our coats down before the King, we will be throwing ourselves down before the throne, worshiping Him forever.

The Players

When I discovered that there will be music in Heaven, I was also interested to learn that the music will not only be vocal, but instrumental as well. Not only will there be singing in Heaven, but there will be instruments of music. In fact, everyone in Heaven will be playing harps:

*And I saw as it were a sea of glass mingled with fire: and them that had gotten the victory over the beast, and over his image, and over his mark, and over the number of his name, stand on the sea of glass, having the **harps** of God. And they **sing** the **song of Moses** the servant of God, and the **song of the Lamb**, saying, Great and marvelous are Thy works, Lord God Almighty; just and true are Thy ways, thou King of saints* (Revelation 15:2-3, emphasis mine).

Whom did John see playing harps in Heaven? All the overcomers who had gotten victory over the beast (the antichrist system) and had not received the mark of the number of the beast.

They were musicians. The Bible is also very careful to mention that these overcomers were singers. In fact, John mentioned two of the songs they were singing: the "Song of Moses" and the "Song of the Lamb." Praise the Lord! Not just those musically inclined here on earth will be playing instruments and singing, but everyone who overcomes the world, the flesh, and the devil will be singing also.

More Musicians in Heaven

John also witnessed another group of people in Heaven: "And I heard a voice from heaven, as the voice of many waters, and as the voice of a great thunder" (Rev. 14:2a).

Notice the tremendous volume of audible worship that John heard. He compared it to the roar of many waterfalls. He didn't know the sound of a plane breaking the sound barrier, or atomic blasts, or the roar of a jackhammer. But he knew the volume of roaring waterfalls and the explosive sound of thunder.

*I heard the voice of **harpers** harping with their **harps**: and they **sung** as it were a new song before the throne, and before the four beasts, and the elders: and no man could learn that song but the hundred and forty and four thousand, which were redeemed from the earth* (Revelation 14:2b-3, emphasis mine).

This group of 144,000 will also be musicians, playing harps. And they will be singing *a new song*. As a songwriter, this excites me. We will be singing in the Spirit a new song before the throne, making up the lyrics and the melody as we are inspired by the presence of Almighty God. We will behold the beauty of Jesus and reflect His attributes in transcendent spontaneous songs of worship. Note that these will be new songs, not songs of the church or songs written by others. We will sing our own compositions in Heaven, and do so endlessly.

God mentions the playing of instruments in Heaven a third time in the Book of Revelation. Because *three* is a spiritually perfect number, it is exciting to know that God mentions music three times in the vision to John, showing us that music is part of the perfect worship in Heaven. Musician, be encouraged. God considers your talents and abilities important enough to be included as one of the forms of worship in Heaven. Shy and timid singer, stand up tall and rejoice with a loud voice for God has chosen your ministry to be used in worship before the throne of the Lamb forever and ever.

> *Now when He had taken the scroll, the four living creatures and the twenty-four elders fell down before the Lamb, each having a harp, and golden bowls full of incense, which are the prayers of the saints. And they sang a new song, saying: "You are worthy to take the scroll, and to open its seals; for You were slain, and have redeemed us to God by Your blood out of every tribe and tongue and people and nation, and have made us kings and priests to our God; and we shall reign on the earth"* (Revelation 5:8-10 NKJ).

Every one of the four beasts and twenty-four elders will have harps. They will be musicians along with the 144,000 and all the overcomers. What an orchestra! And the choir will be just as large because all of them, including the four beasts and twenty-four elders, will sing a new song. The Bible records the lyrics of the song:

> *And I beheld, and I heard the voice of many angels round about the throne and the beasts and the elders: and the number of them was ten thousand times ten thousand, and thousands of thousands; saying with a loud voice, Worthy is the Lamb that was slain to receive power, and riches, and wisdom, and strength, and honour, and glory, and blessing* (Revelation 5:11-12).

The Choir and Orchestra

I can hear that great multitude of millions and millions of worshipers. It is a roar of exaltation and veneration to the Lord of Heaven and earth. What an angelic choir! What sweet orchestration! What a blend of musical instruments and voices from every tribe, nation, people, and language! What a sound! No wonder John said it sounded like, not ordinary thunder, but *great* thunder.

I have been in services of about thirty thousand people with their hands raised, worshiping the Lord out loud with their voices lifted up in praise. And there was a tremendous roar in that auditorium. Can you imagine the awesome praise that will ascend to God from a multitude of millions before the throne, not to mention the animals.

Is it possible that animals will praise the Lord?

*And **every creature** which is in heaven, and on the earth, and under the earth, and such as are in the sea, and **all that are in them**, heard I [John] saying, Blessing, and honour, and glory, and power be unto Him that sitteth upon the throne, and unto the Lamb for ever and ever* (Revelation 5:13).

The preceeding Scripture includes the birds, deer, earthworms, and whales. It includes all that are in the heavens, on the earth, under the earth, and in the sea. Even creation will be singing praise to God. Even creation is involved in the powerful ministry of music.

And the four beasts said, Amen. And the four and twenty elders fell down and worshiped Him that liveth for ever and ever (Revelation 5:14).

Everyone and everything will end in worship to Jesus. This scene in Heaven of worship and praise to the One we love will continue for eternity, and you and I will be part of it.

Music Ministers Wanted!

In the first chapter of this book, we discovered that lucifer fell from Heaven because of his rebellion and pride. When he fell, his ministry of music also fell with him, leaving a music minister's vacancy in Heaven. No longer is there someone who leads the angelic hosts in worship to God the Father. Who will be the anointed cherub that will cover the throne of God? Or will anyone fill this position? The Church has been selected to fill the vacancy left by lucifer. We, the redeemed of the Lord, are going to lead all angels, seraphim and cherubim, and all of creation, in worship to God, with singing and playing on the harps. We, the Bride of Christ, are going to stand before the throne reunited with our Beloved, singing love songs for eternity, telling Him how much we love Him, singing of His majesty and beauty. With our musical instruments we will accompany the angelic choirs as they sing the "Song of Moses" and the "Song of the Lamb." With a new body that will worship longer and sing better and with clear and perfect tone and pitch, our voices will tell of His great salvation and laud Him in the Heavens. All the universe will once again ring with harmonious music, as it did in the beginning, "when the morning stars sang together, and all the sons of God shouted for joy" (Job 38:7).

The ministry of music is a beautiful and powerful one. God has seen fit that it be present in the beginning, and that it be restored once again to end all things. The accounts of music ministry in the Old and New Testaments are numerous. There are hundreds of Scriptures that give us insight as to what God requires. I challenge you, as a musician, singer, songwriter, or arranger, to thoroughly examine the Word of God regarding your ministry. If you have been called of God to minister in music, find out what God expects of you and what responsibilities are placed on you as a priest (minister or servant) in God's house.

God has given you that talent and ability not to play and sing for a living, or for your own pleasure, but to worship the Lord. Although it would be a great honor if you were asked to play for the queen of England in Buckingham Palace or for the President of the United States in the White House, there is no greater honor and privilege than to be invited to play in the courts of His Majesty King Jesus.

God has given you that musical talent to worship Him. Pick up that violin or trombone that you haven't played for a while, dust it off, and use it to praise the Lord! Take the musical instrument that God has given you and discipline yourself to practice, so that you can excel on it. God has commanded us to play skillfully with a loud noise. He wants us to play to the very best of our ability. Give yourself to your God and to His music. It is a ministry, not just entertainment or accompaniment. You are more than a backup musician or session player. You are touching God when you play and sing for His ears only. Music is not a preliminary to the sermon. It is an integral part of each service, divinely appointed by God as a ministry, or service, of praise unto Him. Take your music seriously. God has called you as a priest to minister before Him. For throughout eternity we are going to praise the Lord with loud singing and joyful worship on our instruments.

Chapter Twelve

Music and Praise

One of the foundational aspects of praise is music. Music and praise are closely connected as an expression of God's Kingdom. It is not only the method by which God wants us to come into His presence,[1] but also the form of praise God emphasizes the most in Scripture. We are instructed more often to sing or play praise than to shout or speak praise.

The spirit of praise is a spirit of song. It may find expression in other ways—in sacrifice,[2] or testimony,[3] or prayer[4]—but it finds its most natural and its fullest utterance in lyrical and musical forms. When God fills the heart with praise, He puts a new song into the mouth. The Book of Psalms is proof of this for the Old Testament. And when we read the New Testament, we find the

1.   See Ps. 100:2.
2.   See Lev. 7:13.
3.   See Ps. 66:16.
4.   See Col. 1:3.

same—higher moods of praise express themselves in bursts of song for men and angels, for the Church on earth, and for the Church in Heaven.[5] Finally, in both the Old and New Testaments, the spirit of song gives birth to ordered modes of public praise. In their earlier expressions, the praises of Israel were joyful outbursts in which song was mingled with shouting and dancing to a rude accompaniment of timbrels and trumpets.[6]

Zamar With a Guitar

Several Hebrew words in the Bible are translated "praise" but have a meaning involving music. One of these words is *zamar*. "It is good to *zamar* unto our God" (Ps. 147:1, emphasis mine). This word means to sing while playing a stringed instrument. The word *praise* in the English language is so generic and many people have their own definition of what *praise* means, but in Hebrew the word is more specific. To some people, *praise* means clapping or shouting; to others, proclamations of appreciation. However, when the Holy Spirit moved upon the prophets of old, one of the words He chose to communicate the idea of praise was this word *zamar*.

There are times when we can shout our praise, clap in praise, lift hands in praise, dance in praise. But God says it is good to sing and play a stringed instrument in praise. "I will praise the name of God with a song, and will magnify Him with thanksgiving. This also shall please the Lord better than an ox or bullock that hath horns and hoofs" (Ps. 69:30-31).

Tehillah—Where God Inhabits

The second Hebrew word that involves music is *tehillah*.[7] It means to laud the Divine in song, a hymn or praise. It has connected

---

5. See Lk. 2:14; Eph. 5:19; Col. 3:16; Rev. 5:9; 14:3; 15:3.

6. *International Standard Bible Encyclopaedia*, Electronic Database (Biblesoft, 1996).

7. James Strong, *Strong's Exhaustive Concordance of the Bible* (Peabody, MA: Hendrickson Publishers, n.d.), **tehillah** (#8416)—praise, a song or a hymn of praise.

with it the idea of a new or spontaneous song. We find further definition by the way the word is used in context in Scripture.

"And He hath put a new song in my mouth, even praise [*tehillah*] to our God" (Ps. 40:3a). It is a fresh song that the Lord has put in our mouth. The connection is given here that the new song is *tehillah*. It is an unrehearsed song. It is not on any CD, or in any songbook. There is no lead sheet or transparency for this song, because it doesn't exist until you begin to sing it.

This word is used in another fundamental Scripture on the principle of praise: "But You are holy, enthroned in the praises of Israel" (Ps. 22:3 NKJ). "Enthroned" here means to dwell, remain, sit or abide.[8] God doesn't dwell in just any praise (because there are many expressions of praise), but He promised to dwell in *tehillah* praise. He dwells in the spontaneous songs of His people. It is what some call "singing in the spirit" or the "sacrifice of praise." It is a spontaneous song with no real pattern—a rambling song or chant. It is what happens among the congregation when a known song is finished and there is a spontaneous outburst in song by many worshipers. There may be hundreds of melodies all sung at the same time to God. It is what the author of the Book of Revelation calls "the sound of many waters." This is *tehillah*. It is the sound of Heaven. It is the music in which God dwells.

This type of music praise (*tehillah*) is "power music" because the Divine dwells in it. I am not satisfied with only singing songs *about God* or testimonial songs *of God*, but I want to sing songs *to God* in which He shows up in the middle of the song. I want to sing songs in which the Divine is manifested. When the power of God's presence is near, supernatural things can happen—the healing of the sick,[9] demonic deliverance,[10] prophetic utterance,[11] and

---

8.   *Strong's*, **enthroned** (#3427).
9.   See 1 Sam. 16:23.
10. See 1 Sam. 16:23.
11. See 2 Kings 3:15.

people unable to stand.[12] Anyone can vocalize a pleasant song. Anyone can sing special music and move people. Nice anointed specials are plenteous. However, few sing such that God moves and His power is manifested in the physical realm. Now that is "power music."

"Enter into His gates with thanksgiving, and into His courts with praise [*tehillah*]" (Ps. 100:4a). This kind of music is the gate that ushers us into the King's courts. Of Zion it is said, "You will call your walls salvation, and your gates praise [*tehillah*]" (Is. 60:18b NAS). The presence of God at the entrance of Zion is called praise. The perimeter is salvation. If you are saved and acknowledge Jesus Christ as your Lord and Savior, then you qualify to enter a gate called praise. This gate is more than just an entrance. It is a gate that can open or close the entrance. You can open or shut the gate of praise by your will. If you make a choice to enter into praise, it will give you access (open) to the presence of the Lord. If you choose not to praise, the gate remains closed and you will not enter into His courts. "Go through, go through the gates," Isaiah encourages in Isaiah 62:10a. "Lift up your heads, O ye gates; and be ye lifted up, ye everlasting doors; and the King of glory shall come in" (Ps. 24:7). Musical praise is a very special form of music. It is a main purpose for which music was created.

The Genesis of Music

For by Him were all things created, that are in heaven, and that are in earth, visible and invisible, whether they be thrones, or dominions, or principalities, or powers: all things were created by Him, and for Him (Colossians 1:16, emphasis mine).

Christ created all things, which includes music, and He created it for a very specific purpose, not for our pleasure, not for evangelism, not for Christians, not for missionary work; He created music for Himself. Music was created for praise and worship. The

---

12.   See 2 Chron. 5:13-14.

music He desires the most is praise because He will inhabit it when we sing it.

Music was created for God, not for you or me. "Thou art worthy, O Lord, to receive glory and honour and power: for Thou hast created *all* things, and *for Thy pleasure* they are and were created" (Rev. 4:11, emphasis mine). God's intention when He said, "Let there be light,"[13] was to make musical praise, not to any other god or power, but to Himself.

Praise is released and expanded with music. There are many ways to praise, as we mentioned earlier, but God emphasizes the singing of praise. Over 280 times in the Bible we are commanded to sing unto the Lord (praise). Most of the time we are told to sing a new song. The Bible never says sing an old song, but always a new song. God loves spontaneous music that comes from our heart because that is praise. Old songs can be memorized, rehearsed, and mechanically performed; but a new song has life, is full of meaningful expression, and is fresh. The first time you sing a song you bring into existence a musical expression of what you are feeling inside. Because our Heavenly Father is relational, He wants to hear your personal song. There is a freshness there that God enjoys.

Music and praise are profoundly linked together throughout Scripture and so they should be in our lives. Sing your spontaneous praise and expect to encounter God's presence. Let your music be more than a nice or "hot" arrangement. Let it be "power music."

I challenge you to study the theology of music. Use this book as a starting point. The Appendix lists Scripture references that mention instruments and musical terms. I trust that as you study to show yourself approved unto God, you will experience a rebirth of music in your life.

---

13. Music is part of the light spectrum because it is sound.

Appendix

A List of Scriptures About Music in the Bible

(1028 mentions in Scripture)

Musical Instruments

1. Bells
Exodus 28:33,34
Exodus 39:25,26
Zechariah 14:20

2. Brass
1 Corinthians 13:1

3. Cornet(s)
2 Samuel 6:5
1 Chronicles 15:28
2 Chronicles 15:14
Psalm 98:6
Daniel 3:5,7,10,15
Hosea 5:8

4. Cymbal(s)
2 Samuel 6:5
1 Chronicles 13:8
1 Chronicles 15:16,19,28
1 Chronicles 16:5,42

1 Chronicles 25:1,6
2 Chronicles 5:12,13
2 Chronicles 29:25
Ezra 3:10
Nehemiah 12:27
Psalm 150:5
1 Corinthians 13:1

5. Dulcimer (a bagpipe)
Daniel 3:5,10,15

6. Flute
Daniel 3:5,7,10,15

7. Harp(s), Harpers
Genesis 4:21
Genesis 31:27
1 Samuel 10:5
1 Samuel 16:16,23
2 Samuel 6:5
1 Kings 10:12
1 Chronicles 13:8
1 Chronicles 15:16,21,28
1 Chronicles 16:5
1 Chronicles 25:1,3,6
2 Chronicles 5:12,15
2 Chronicles 9:11
2 Chronicles 20:28
2 Chronicles 29:25
Nehemiah 12:27
Job 21:12
Job 30:31
Psalm 33:2
Psalm 43:4
Psalm 49:4

Psalm 57:8
Psalm 71:22
Psalm 81:2
Psalm 92:3
Psalm 98:5 (twice)
Psalm 108:2
Psalm 137:2
Psalm 147:7
Psalm 149:3
Psalm 150:3
Isaiah 5:12
Isaiah 16:11
Isaiah 23:16
Isaiah 24:8
Isaiah 30:32
Ezekiel 26:13
Daniel 3:5,7,10,15
1 Corinthians 14:7 (twice)
Revelation 5:8
Revelation 14:2 (twice)
Revelation 15:2
Revelation 18:22

8. Organ(s)

Genesis 4:21
Job 21:12
Job 30:31
Psalm 150:4

9. Pipe(s), Piped, Pipers

1 Samuel 10:5
1 Kings 1:40 (twice)
Isaiah 5:12
Isaiah 30:29
Jeremiah 48:36 (twice)

Ezekiel 28:13
Zechariah 4:2
Zechariah 4:12
Matthew 11:17
Luke 7:32
1 Corinthians 14:7 (twice)
Revelation 18:22

10. Psaltery

1 Samuel 10:5
2 Samuel 6:5
1 Kings 10:12
1 Chronicles 13:8
1 Chronicles 15:16,20,28
1 Chronicles 16:5
1 Chronicles 26:1,6
2 Chronicles 5:12
2 Chronicles 9:11
2 Chronicles 20:28
2 Chronicles 29:25
Nehemiah 12:27
Psalm 33:2
Psalm 57:8
Psalm 71:22
Psalm 81:2
Psalm 92:3
Psalm 108:2
Psalm 144:9
Psalm 150:3
Daniel 3:5,7,10,15

11. Ram's Horns

Joshua 6:4,5,6,8,13

12. Sackbut (a wind instrument)

Daniel 3:5,7,10,15

13. Sheminith (8-stringed lyre)

(octave, deep voices)
1 Chronicles 15:21
Psalm 6 (subtitle)
Psalm 12 (subtitle)

14. Tabret(s) (tambourines)

Genesis 31:27
1 Samuel 10:5
1 Samuel 18:6
Job 17:6
Isaiah 5:12
Isaiah 24:8
Isaiah 30:32
Jeremiah 31:4
Ezekiel 28:13

15. Timbrels (tambourines)

Exodus 15:20 (twice)
Judges 11:34
2 Samuel 6:5
1 Chronicles 13:8
Job 21:12
Psalm 68:25
Psalm 81:2
Psalm 149:3
Psalm 150:4

16. Trumpet(s), Trump, Trumpeters

Exodus 19:13,16,19
Exodus 20:18
Leviticus 23:24
Leviticus 25:9 (twice)
Numbers 10:2,4,8,9,10
Numbers 29:1
Numbers 31:6

Joshua 6:4 (twice)
Joshua 6:5,6,16
Joshua 6:8 (twice)
Joshua 6:9 (twice)
Joshua 6:13 (three times)
Joshua 6:20 (twice)
Judges 3:27
Judges 7:8,16,19,22
Judges 7:18 (twice)
Judges 7:20 (twice)
1 Samuel 13:3
2 Samuel 2:28
2 Samuel 6:15
2 Samuel 15:10
2 Samuel 18:16
2 Samuel 20:1,22
1 Kings 1:34,39,41
2 Kings 9:13
2 Kings 11:14 (twice)
2 Kings 12:13
1 Chronicles 13:8
1 Chronicles 15:24,28
1 Chronicles 16:6,42
2 Chronicles 5:12
2 Chronicles 5:13 (twice)
2 Chronicles 7:6
2 Chronicles 13:12,14
2 Chronicles 15:14
2 Chronicles 20:28
2 Chronicles 23:13 (twice)
2 Chronicles 29:26,27,28
Ezra 3:10
Nehemiah 4:18,20
Nehemiah 12:35,41
Job 39:24,25
Psalm 47:5
Psalm 81:3

Psalm 98:6
Psalm 150:3
Isaiah 18:3
Isaiah 27:13
Isaiah 58:1
Jeremiah 4:5,19,21
Jeremiah 6:1,17
Jeremiah 42:14
Jeremiah 51:27
Ezekiel 7:14
Ezekiel 33:3,4,5,6
Hosea 5:8
Hosea 8:1
Joel 2:1,15
Amos 2:2
Amos 3:6
Zephaniah 1:16
Zechariah 9:14
Matthew 6:2
Matthew 24:31
1 Corinthians 14:8
1 Corinthians 15:52 (twice)
1 Thessalonians 4:16
Hebrews 12:19
Revelation 1:10
Revelation 4:1
Revelation 8:2,6,13
Revelation 9:14
Revelation 18:22

17. Viol(s)

Isaiah 5:12
Isaiah 14:11
Amos 5:23
Amos 6:5

Musical Terms

1. Alamoth (soprano female voices)
1 Chronicles 15:20
Psalm 46 (subtitle)

2. Altascheth ("destroy not" —maybe opening lyrics of popular song)
Psalm 57 (subtitle)
Psalm 58 (subtitle)
Psalm 59 (subtitle)
Psalm 75 (subtitle)

3. Gittith (harmony)
Psalm 8 (subtitle)
Psalm 81 (subtitle)
Psalm 84 (subtitle)

4. Higgaion (muted music[1])
Psalm 9:16

5. Hymns
Matthew 26:30

---

1.   Jerusalem Bible.

Mark 14:26
Ephesians 5:19
Colossians 3:16

6. Jonathelemrechokim

Psalm 56 (subtitle)

7. Leannoth (sing loudly to create attention)

Psalm 88 (subtitle)

8. Mahalath (title or word of a popular song)

Psalm 53 (subtitle)
Psalm 88 (subtitle)

9. Maschil

Psalm 32 (subtitle)
Psalm 42 (subtitle)
Psalm 44 (subtitle)
Psalm 45 (subtitle)
Psalm 52 (subtitle)
Psalm 53 (subtitle)
Psalm 54 (subtitle)
Psalm 55 (subtitle)
Psalm 74 (subtitle)
Psalm 78 (subtitle)
Psalm 88 (subtitle)
Psalm 89 (subtitle)
Psalm 142 (subtitle)

10. Massa—(an utterance, especially singing—translated burden[2])

Nehemiah 1:1
Proverbs 30:1

---

2.   *Strong's*, #4853.

Proverbs 31:1
Isaiah 13:1
Isaiah 14:28
Isaiah 15:1
Isaiah 17:1
Isaiah 19:1
Isaiah 21:1,11,13
Isaiah 22:1,25
Isaiah 23:1
Isaiah 30:6
Isaiah 46:1,2
Ezekiel 12:10
Hosea 8:10
Habakkuk 1:1
Zechariah 9:1
Zechariah 12:1
Malachi 1:1

11. Melody

Isaiah 23:16
Isaiah 51:3
Amos 5:23
Ephesians 5:19

12. Minstrels (players of stringed instruments)

2 Kings 3:15 (twice)
Matthew 9:23

13. Music, Musical, Musician(s)

1 Samuel 18:6
1 Chronicles 15:16
1 Chronicles 16:42
2 Chronicles 5:13
2 Chronicles 7:6
2 Chronicles 23:13

2 Chronicles 34:12
Nehemiah 12:36
Psalm 4 (subtitle)
Psalm 5 (subtitle)
Psalm 6 (subtitle)
Psalm 8 (subtitle)
Psalm 9 (subtitle)
Psalm 11 (subtitle)
Psalm 12 (subtitle)
Psalm 13 (subtitle)
Psalm 14 (subtitle)
Psalm 18 (subtitle)
Psalm 19 (subtitle)
Psalm 20 (subtitle)
Psalm 21 (subtitle)
Psalm 22 (subtitle)
Psalm 31 (subtitle)
Psalm 36 (subtitle)
Psalm 39 (subtitle)
Psalm 40 (subtitle)
Psalm 41 (subtitle)
Psalm 42 (subtitle)
Psalm 44 (subtitle)
Psalm 45 (subtitle)
Psalm 46 (subtitle)
Psalm 47 (subtitle)
Psalm 49 (subtitle)
Psalm 51 (subtitle)
Psalm 52 (subtitle)
Psalm 53 (subtitle)
Psalm 54 (subtitle)
Psalm 55 (subtitle)
Psalm 56 (subtitle)
Psalm 57 (subtitle)
Psalm 58 (subtitle)
Psalm 59 (subtitle)

Psalm 60 (subtitle)
Psalm 61 (subtitle)
Psalm 62 (subtitle)
Psalm 64 (subtitle)
Psalm 65 (subtitle)
Psalm 66 (subtitle)
Psalm 67 (subtitle)
Psalm 68 (subtitle)
Psalm 69 (subtitle)
Psalm 70 (subtitle)
Psalm 75 (subtitle)
Psalm 76 (subtitle)
Psalm 77 (subtitle)
Psalm 80 (subtitle)
Psalm 81 (subtitle)
Psalm 84 (subtitle)
Psalm 85 (subtitle)
Psalm 88 (subtitle)
Psalm 109 (subtitle)
Psalm 139 (subtitle)
Psalm 140 (subtitle)
Ecclesiastes 2:8
Ecclesiastes 12:4
Lamentations 3:63
Lamentations 5:14
Daniel 3:5,7,10,15
Daniel 6:18
Amos 6:5
Luke 15:25
Revelation 18:22

14. Muthlabben ("die for the son;" title of a popular song)

Psalm 9 (subtitle)

15. Naba (to speak or sing by inspiration[3]; translated "prophecy" or "prophet")

Numbers 11:25,26

1 Samuel 10:5,6,10,11,13,

1 Samuel 18:10

1 Samuel 19:20,21,23,24

1 Kings 18:29

1 Kings 22:8,10,12,18

1 Chronicles 25:1-3

2 Chronicles 18:7,9,11,27

2 Chronicles 20:37

Psalm 19:2

Psalm 78:2

Psalm 94:4

Psalm 119:171

Psalm 145:7

Jeremiah 2:8

Jeremiah 5:31

Jeremiah 11:21

Jeremiah 14:14,15,16

Jeremiah 19:14

Jeremiah 20:1,6

Jeremiah 23:13,16,21,25,26,32

Jeremiah 25:13,30

Jeremiah 26:9,11,12,18,20

Jeremiah 27:10,14,16

Jeremiah 27:15 (twice)

Jeremiah 28:6,8,9

Jeremiah 29:9,21,31

Jeremiah 32:3

Jeremiah 37:19

Ezekiel 4:7

Ezekiel 6:2

Ezekiel 11:4,13

---

3.   *Strong's*, #5012.

Ezekiel 12:27
Ezekiel 13:16,17
Ezekiel 20:46
Ezekiel 21:2,9,14,28
Ezekiel 25:2
Ezekiel 28:21
Ezekiel 29:2
Ezekiel 30:2
Ezekiel 34:2
Ezekiel 35:2
Ezekiel 36:1,3,6
Ezekiel 37:4,7,9,12
Ezekiel 38:2,14,17
Ezekiel 39:1
Joel 2:28
Amos 2:12
Amos 3:8
Amos 7:12,13,15,16
Zechariah 13:3,4

16. Neginah, or Neginoth (stringed instrument or harps[4])

Psalm 4 (subtitle)
Psalm 6 (subtitle)
Psalm 54 (subtitle)
Psalm 55 (subtitle)
Psalm 61 (subtitle)
Psalm 67 (subtitle)
Psalm 76 (subtitle)

17. Nehiloth (flute[5] or wind instruments[6])

Psalm 5 (subtitle)

---

4.   An American Translation (Smith and Godspeed).
5.   An American Translation (Smith and Godspeed).
6.   American Baptist Publication Society.

18. Piper(s), Piped

1 Samuel 19:9
1 Kings 1:40
2 Kings 3:15
Luke 7:32
1 Corinthians 13:8
1 Corinthians 14:7
Revelation 18:22

19. Played (musical instruments)

1 Samuel 16:23
1 Samuel 18:7

20. Player(s) (of musical instruments)

1 Samuel 6:21
1 Samuel 16:16,17,18,23
1 Samuel 18:10
1 Samuel 19:9
2 Kings 3:15
1 Chronicles 15:29
Psalm 33:3
Psalm 68:25 (twice)
Psalm 87:7
Ezekiel 33:32

21. Psalm(s), Psalmist

2 Samuel 23:1
1 Chronicles 16:7,9
Psalm 3 (subtitle)
Psalm 4 (subtitle)
Psalm 5 (subtitle)
Psalm 6 (subtitle)
Psalm 8 (subtitle)
Psalm 9 (subtitle)
Psalm 11 (subtitle)

Psalm 12 (subtitle)
Psalm 13 (subtitle)
Psalm 14 (subtitle)
Psalm 15 (subtitle)
Psalm 18 (subtitle)
Psalm 19 (subtitle)
Psalm 20 (subtitle)
Psalm 21 (subtitle)
Psalm 22 (subtitle)
Psalm 23 (subtitle)
Psalm 24 (subtitle)
Psalm 25 (subtitle)
Psalm 26 (subtitle)
Psalm 27 (subtitle)
Psalm 28 (subtitle)
Psalm 29 (subtitle)
Psalm 30 (subtitle)
Psalm 31 (subtitle)
Psalm 32 (subtitle)
Psalm 34 (subtitle)
Psalm 35 (subtitle)
Psalm 36 (subtitle)
Psalm 37 (subtitle)
Psalm 38 (subtitle)
Psalm 39 (subtitle)
Psalm 40 (subtitle)
Psalm 41 (subtitle)
Psalm 47 (subtitle)
Psalm 48 (subtitle)
Psalm 49 (subtitle)
Psalm 50 (subtitle)
Psalm 51 (subtitle)
Psalm 52 (subtitle)
Psalm 53 (subtitle)
Psalm 54 (subtitle)
Psalm 55 (subtitle)

Psalm 61 (subtitle)
Psalm 62 (subtitle)
Psalm 63 (subtitle)
Psalm 64 (subtitle)
Psalm 65 (subtitle)
Psalm 66 (subtitle)
Psalm 67 (subtitle)
Psalm 68 (subtitle)
Psalm 69 (subtitle)
Psalm 70 (subtitle)
Psalm 72 (subtitle)
Psalm 73 (subtitle)
Psalm 75 (subtitle)
Psalm 76 (subtitle)
Psalm 77 (subtitle)
Psalm 79 (subtitle)
Psalm 80 (subtitle)
Psalm 81 (subtitle)
Psalm 81:2
Psalm 82 (subtitle)
Psalm 83 (subtitle)
Psalm 84 (subtitle)
Psalm 85 (subtitle)
Psalm 87 (subtitle)
Psalm 88 (subtitle)
Psalm 92 (subtitle)
Psalm 95:2
Psalm 98 (subtitle)
Psalm 98:5
Psalm 100 (subtitle)
Psalm 101 (subtitle)
Psalm 103 (subtitle)
Psalm 105:2
Psalm 108 (subtitle)
Psalm 109 (subtitle)
Psalm 110 (subtitle)

Psalm 138 (subtitle)
Psalm 139 (subtitle)
Psalm 140 (subtitle)
Psalm 141 (subtitle)
Psalm 143 (subtitle)
Psalm 144 (subtitle)
Psalm 145 (subtitle)
Luke 20:42
Luke 24:44
Acts 1:20
Acts 13:33,35
1 Corinthians 14:26
Ephesians 5:19
Colossians 3:16
James 5:13

22. Sang, Sing, Singed, Singeth, Singer(s), Singing, Song(s), Sung

Genesis 31:27
Exodus 15:1(twice)
Exodus 15:21
Exodus 32:18
Numbers 21:17 (twice)
Judges 5:1,12
Judges 5:3 (twice)
1 Samuel 18:6
1 Samuel 21:11
1 Samuel 29:5
2 Samuel 19:35 (twice)
2 Samuel 22:1,50
1 Kings 4:32
1 Kings 10:12
1 Chronicles 6:31,32,33
1 Chronicles 9:33
1 Chronicles 13:8

1 Chronicles 15:16,19
1 Chronicles 15:22 (twice)
1 Chronicles 15:27 (three times)
1 Chronicles 16:9,23,33
1 Chronicles 25:6,7
2 Chronicles 5:12,13
2 Chronicles 9:11
2 Chronicles 20:21,22
2 Chronicles 23:13 (twice)
2 Chronicles 23:18
2 Chronicles 29:27,30
2 Chronicles 29:28 (twice)
2 Chronicles 30:21
2 Chronicles 35:15
2 Chronicles 35:25 (twice)
Ezra 2:41,70
Ezra 2:65 (twice)
Ezra 3:11
Ezra 7:7,24
Ezra 10:24
Nehemiah 7:1,44,73
Nehemiah 7:67 (twice)
Nehemiah 10:28,39
Nehemiah 11:22,23
Nehemiah 12:27,28,29,45,46,47
Nehemiah 12:42,46 (twice)
Nehemiah 13:5,10
Job 29:13
Job 30:9
Job 35:10
Job 38:7
Psalm 7 (subtitle)
Psalm 7:17
Psalm 9:2,11
Psalm 13:6
Psalm 18:49

Psalm 21:13
Psalm 27:6 (twice)
Psalm 28:7
Psalm 30:4,12
Psalm 32:7
Psalm 33:2
Psalm 33:3 (twice)
Psalm 40:3
Psalm 42:8
Psalm 45 (subtitle)
Psalm 46 (subtitle)
Psalm 47:6 (four times)
Psalm 47:7
Psalm 48 (subtitle)
Psalm 51:14
Psalm 57:7,9
Psalm 59:16 (twice)
Psalm 59:17
Psalm 61:8
Psalm 65:13
Psalm 66:2
Psalm 66:4 (twice)
Psalm 67:4
Psalm 68:4,32 (twice)
Psalm 68:25
Psalm 69:12,30
Psalm 71:22,23
Psalm 75:9
Psalm 76 (subtitle)
Psalm 77:6
Psalm 81:1
Psalm 83 (subtitle)
Psalm 87:7
Psalm 88 (subtitle)
Psalm 89:1,17
Psalm 92:1

Psalm 95:1
Psalm 96:1 (three times)
Psalm 96:2
Psalm 98:1 (three times)
Psalm 98:4,5
Psalm 100:2
Psalm 101:1 (twice)
Psalm 104:12
Psalm 104:33 (twice)
Psalm 105:2 (twice)
Psalm 105:3
Psalm 106:12
Psalm 108:1,3
Psalm 118:14
Psalm 119:54
Psalm 120 (subtitle)
Psalm 121 (subtitle)
Psalm 122 (subtitle)
Psalm 123 (subtitle)
Psalm 124 (subtitle)
Psalm 125 (subtitle)
Psalm 126 (subtitle)
Psalm 126:2
Psalm 127 (subtitle)
Psalm 128 (subtitle)
Psalm 129 (subtitle)
Psalm 130 (subtitle)
Psalm 131 (subtitle)
Psalm 132 (subtitle)
Psalm 133 (subtitle)
Psalm 134 (subtitle)
Psalm 135:3
Psalm 137:3 (three times)
Psalm 137:4 (twice)
Psalm 138:1,5
Psalm 144:9

Psalm 145:7
Psalm 146:2
Psalm 147:1
Psalm 147:7 (three times)
Psalm 149:1 (twice)
Psalm 149:3,5
Proverbs 25:20 (twice)
Proverbs 29:6
Song of Solomon 1:1 (twice)
Song of Solomon 2:12
Ecclesiastes 2:8 (twice)
Ecclesiastes 7:5
Isaiah 5:1 (twice)
Isaiah 12:2,5
Isaiah 14:7
Isaiah 16:10
Isaiah 23:15,16 (twice)
Isaiah 24:9,14,16
Isaiah 26:1
Isaiah 26:19 (twice)
Isaiah 27:2
Isaiah 30:29
Isaiah 35:2,6,10
Isaiah 38:20 (twice)
Isaiah 42:10 (twice)
Isaiah 42:11
Isaiah 44:23
Isaiah 48:20
Isaiah 49:13 (twice)
Isaiah 51:11
Isaiah 52:8,9
Isaiah 54:1 (twice)
Isaiah 55:12
Isaiah 65:14
Jeremiah 20:13
Jeremiah 31:7,12

Jeremiah 15:48
Lamentations 3:14
Ezekiel 26:13
Ezekiel 27:25,66
Ezekiel 33:32
Ezekiel 40:44
Daniel 3:27
Hosea 2:15
Amos 5:23
Amos 8:3,10
Habakkuk 3:19
Zephaniah 2:14
Zephaniah 3:14,17
Zechariah 2:10
Matthew 26:30
Mark 14:26
Acts 16:25
Romans 15:9
1 Corinthians 14:15 (twice)
Ephesians 5:19 (twice)
Colossians 3:16 (twice)
Hebrews 2:12
James 5:13
Revelation 5:9 (twice)
Revelation 14:3 (three times)
Revelation 15:3 (twice)

23. Selah (vocal pause, change instrumentation, modulate, or musical interlude)

Joshua 15:38
2 Kings 14:7
Psalm 3:2,4,8
Psalm 4:2,4
Psalm 7:5
Psalm 9:16,20

Psalm 20:3
Psalm 21:2
Psalm 24:6,10
Psalm 32:4,5,7
Psalm 39:5,11
Psalm 44:8
Psalm 46:3,7,11
Psalm 47:4,8
Psalm 48:8
Psalm 49:13,15
Psalm 50:6
Psalm 52:3,5
Psalm 54:3
Psalm 55:7,19
Psalm 57:3,6
Psalm 59:5,13
Psalm 60:4
Psalm 61:4
Psalm 62:4,8
Psalm 66:4,7,15
Psalm 67:1,4
Psalm 68:7,19,32
Psalm 75:3
Psalm 76:3,9
Psalm 77:3,9,15
Psalm 81:7
Psalm 82:2
Psalm 83:8
Psalm 84:4,8
Psalm 85:2
Psalm 87:3,6
Psalm 88:7,10
Psalm 89:4,37,45,48
Psalm 140:3,5,8
Psalm 143:6
Habakkuk 3:3,9,13

24. Shiggaion, Shigionoth (various songs or rambling lyric)

Psalm 7 (subtitle)
Habakkuk 3:1

25. Shoshannim or Shoshannimeduth (a musical term)

Psalm 45 (subtitle)
Psalm 69 (subtitle)
Psalm 80 (subtitle)

26. Shushaneduth (a musical term)

Psalm 60 (subtitle)

RESOURCES AND REFERENCES

Best, Harold. *Music Through the Eyes of Faith*. Harper Collins, 1993.

Blomgren, David. *Song of the Lord*. Portland, OR. Bible Press, 1978.

Gaynor, Mitchell L. *The Sounds of Healing*. Broadway, New York, NY, 1999.

Grein, Janny. *Called, Appointed, Anointed*. Tulsa, OK. Praise Books, 1981.

International Standard Bible Encyclopaedia. Electronic Database. Biblesoft, 1996.

Larson, Bob. *Rock*. Wheaton, IL. Tyndale House, 1980.

Law, Terry. *The Power of Praise and Worship*. Tulsa, OK. Victory House Publishers, 1985

Robertson. *Word Pictures in the New Testament*. Biblesoft, 1997.

Strong, James. *Strong's Exhaustive Concordance of the Bible*. Peabody, MA. Hendrickson Publishers, n.d.

Taylor, Jack R. *The Hallelujah Factor*. Nashville, TN. Broadman Press, 1983.

Thayer's Bible Dictionary. Public domain.

Truscott, Graham. *The Power of His Presence*. San Diego, CA. Restoration Temple, 1969.

Books by LaMar Boschman

A Passion for His Presence

Discover what the presence of God is and how to live in His presence daily.

Real Men Worship

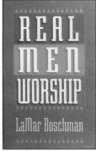

Learn how to be a real man who is a real worshiper.

Heart of Worship

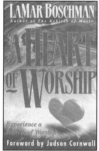

For those looking for worship renewal in their personal life as well as the local church.

The Rebirth of Music

Explore the real meaning and purpose of music. Approximately 1,000 Scriptures on music.

Future Worship

What will worship look like as we enter the next century? This book explores current worship trends and where they will take us in the future.

Prophetic Song

Learn how to prophesy through song and through musical instruments.

To order books call:
1-800-627-0923
www.lamarboschman.com

Resources from
The Worship Institute

The Worship Leaders' Training Course 1–3

Becoming an effective worship leader takes more than music. This powerful resource series has touched hundreds of worship leaders around the country. LaMar Boschman and other leaders share how to prepare, empower, and increase your effectiveness as a worship leader. Available in audio or video with syllabus.

The Worship Team Training Course 1–3

This unique course will equip and inspire your worship team. From playing together to praying together you will learn how to empower your worship team as never before. Seven leading worship ministers instruct you and your worship team. Each volume contains 4 — 45 minute videos.

Plan now to attend the International Worship Institute. This five-day master worship intensive is held annually in Dallas/Ft. Worth and is attended by hundreds of worship ministers from around the world.

For a free catalog, or more information contact:
The Worship Institute
P.O. Box 130, Bedford, Texas   76095
www.worshipinstitute.com
1-800-627-0923

Destiny Image titles
you will enjoy reading

Exciting titles
by Tommy Tenney

Exciting titles
by Don Nori

NO MORE SOUR GRAPES

Who among us wants our children to be free from the struggles we have had to bear? Who among us wants the lives of our children to be full of victory and love for their Lord? Who among us wants the hard-earned lessons from our lives given freely to our children? All these are not only possible, they are also God's will. You can be one of those who share the excitement and joy of seeing your children step into the destiny God has for them. If you answered "yes" to these questions, the pages of this book are full of hope and help for you and others just like you.
ISBN 0-7684-2037-7

THE POWER OF BROKENNESS

Accepting Brokenness is a must for becoming a true vessel of the Lord, and is a stepping-stone to revival in our hearts, our homes, and our churches. Brokenness alone brings us to the wonderful revelation of how deep and great our Lord's mercy really is. Join this companion who leads us through the darkest of nights. Discover the *Power of Brokenness*.
ISBN 1-56043-178-4

THE ANGEL AND THE JUDGMENT

Few understand the power of our judgments—or the aftermath of the words we speak in thoughtless, emotional pain. In this powerful story about a preacher and an angel, you'll see how the heavens respond and how the earth is changed by the words we utter in secret.
ISBN 1-56043-154-7

HIS MANIFEST PRESENCE

This is a passionate look at God's desire for a people with whom He can have intimate fellowship. Not simply a book on worship, it faces our triumphs as well as our sorrows in relation to God's plan for a dwelling place that is splendid in holiness and love.
ISBN 0-914903-48-9
Also available in Spanish.
ISBN 1-56043-079-6

SECRETS OF THE MOST HOLY PLACE

Here is a prophetic parable you will read again and again. The winds of God are blowing, drawing you to His Life within the Veil of the Most Holy Place. There you begin to see as you experience a depth of relationship your heart has yearned for. This book is a living, dynamic experience with God!
ISBN 1-56043-076-1

HOW TO FIND GOD'S LOVE

Here is a heartwarming story about three people who tell their stories of tragedy, fear, and disease, and how God showed them His love in a real way.
ISBN 0-914903-28-4
Also available in Spanish.
ISBN 1-56043-024-9

Available at your local Christian bookstore.

Exciting titles
by Joseph Garlington